The Rapture is Only the Beginning

THE CHURCH OF THE LEFT BEHIND

A Complete Guide for Survivors Left Behind after
the Rapture and the Second Coming of Jesus Christ

FRANK MAZZ

D1280033

Other books by
Frank Mazzapica

The Unsupervised Man

The Unsupervised Woman

The Touch-Me-Not Woman

Meet the Beasts

Putting Pants Back on the Church

ISBN-13: 978-0-9968715-8-7

Printed in the United States of America

RevMedia Publishing
PO BOX 5172, Kingwood, TX 77325

Dedicated to my son Nathan, for had he not planted the seed to research the truth about the kingdom, the pages of this book would not have seen daylight.

Contents

Foreword

There is no subject in the Bible or the world more intriguing or controversial than the future of the world and the coming Kingdom of God. Many Christians find the prophetic books of Isaiah, Ezekiel, Daniel, and Revelation fascinating, even addicting, although allusive in real meaning. I certainly fall into that category.

Since childhood, I have listened to the best teachers of the day, read countless books on the subject, and searched the Bible from cover to cover on the matter. Still, it remains mostly a mystery to me with far more questions than answers. To some degree, I believe that is the way God intended for it to be.

Daniel was commanded to *"...shut up the words, and seal the book even to the time of the end..."* (Dan. 12:4 KJV). God did not want us to know certain things until they were at hand. Maybe this explains why much of scriptural prophecies concerning the final chapters of God's plan for mankind are shrouded in mystery.

In the New Testament, the disciples ask Jesus about the future of Israel. He replied, "...It is not for you to know times or seasons which the Father has put in His own authority" (Acts 1:7 KJV). Some things, especially relating to exact date-setting, seem to be hidden from our eyes. During the last forty years, we have witnessed one "date setter" after another be proven wrong and forced to revise their predictions.

Nevertheless, we continue to study and believe that every word spoken by the prophets will be fulfilled in exact detail, and the plan of God will be carried out without fail.

"Repent ye therefore and be converted, that your sins may be blotted out, so that times of refreshing may come from the presence of the Lord; and He may send Jesus Christ, which before was preached unto you, whom heaven must receive until the times of restitution of all things, which God hath spoken by the mouth of all His holy prophets since the world began." (Acts 3:19-21 KJV)

With that said, I believe that the Holy Spirit is unlocking portions of the mystery to us in these last days, as much of what was predicted in Scripture is being fulfilled in the world around us. Prophetic scenes viewed hundreds of years ago by profound men of God seemed more like a Stephen Spielberg production than future realities, begging the question of whether the narrative was intended to be figurative or literal. When those scenes are viewed today against the backdrop of global events, a new world order, modern technology, and the development of weapons of mass destruction, etc. we are often compelled to move what previously was thought to be figurative to the literal column. I firmly believe that the closer we get to the fulfillment of a scriptural prophecy, the more readily it will be understood in advance. Even now, age-old mysteries are unfolding with each current event.

Let's take a quick look back at the first coming of Jesus Christ, and see what can be learned to prepare us for the second coming of Jesus Christ.

The first coming of the Messiah was foretold in exact detail by a dozen or more prophets over a period of nearly 4000 years. The Jewish nation was guardian of these prophecies and rehearsed them from generation to generation as the most important aspect of their religion and faith. Yet, when the Messiah actually came, they did not recognize Him. Centuries of study and contemplation had left them in the dark concerning their fulfillment in Jesus. He came and went without their realizing that the One they were looking for was at that moment among them. Paul explained that blindness in part had come to the

Jews. (See Romans 8:25.)

So, the Jews of Jesus' day failed to relate prophecy to current events. Maybe they just couldn't grasp that the things spoken by the prophets were actually coming to pass in their day. Therefore, the Jewish nation rejected the very One they had looked for and committed an enormous sin against God that continues to affect their spiritual and national condition today.

Could that happen to Christians concerning the second coming of Christ?

It's sobering to realize that major prophetic events could be occurring around us in our day and we don't realize it. Maybe even reject them as the Jews did concerning Jesus. This is a day to know the signs of the time and to stay alert to what is happening in the world as it relates to biblical prophecy.

Our future hope is in the second coming of Jesus Christ. Like the Jews, we have an ample supply of scriptural prophecies to guide us into an understanding of that climatic event. Therefore, it is extremely important to search the Scriptures diligently, looking for understanding, always believing that every word spoken by the prophets will be fulfilled and that Jesus will literally return to earth and become the head of all nations. In a sequence of dramatic events, the ultimate Kingdom of God will be established on earth, and the people of God will rule and reign with Him for a thousand years.

"Blessed and holy is he who has part in the first resurrection; on such the second death hath no power, but they shall be priests of God and of Christ, and shall reign with Him a thousand years." (Rev. 20:6 KJV)

At this very moment, cataclysmic events are occurring in alignment with prophetic Scripture. This leads us to believe that the long awaited second coming of Jesus and associated events are soon to occur. This compels us to study the scripture more diligently, to watch for the signs of His coming, and especially to live in a state of readiness. *"Watch therefore, for ye know neither the day nor the hour wherein the Son of Man cometh"* (Matt. 25:13

KJV).

The command to "watch" comes at the end of an extraordinary prophecy concerning the return of Christ. In Matthew 25:1-13, Jesus tells the story of ten virgins who were waiting for a bridegroom to return. Five of them were personally prepared and were received by the bridegroom, while the other five were unprepared and therefore missed the wedding. Five were wise and five were foolish, Jesus said. This story foretells the mindset of church people at the point of His return and strongly suggests that one half will be totally unprepared and left behind. What a disturbing prediction.

As followers of Jesus Christ, we must stay alert, and be ready at all times for His coming lest we become like the Jews who failed to recognize Jesus for who He was, or be like the five foolish virgins who were simply unprepared and missed the very thing they were waiting for.

Author Frank Mazzapica has spent the better part of forty years studying biblical prophecy and preparing the people of God for the end times. I do not know anyone with more overall knowledge and understanding of the subject. I admire the courage and clarity with which he presents this powerful teaching. My prayer is for God to use this phenomenal book to awaken those who are spiritually asleep and better prepare the church for what God is about to do in the earth.

I encourage you to read this book with an open mind and with faith. Afterward, you will be even more determined to walk with God and live in a constant state of readiness for His glorious return.

God bless you,

Bishop Randy Clark

TRIUMPH CHURCH
SOUTHEAST TEXAS

Introduction

This is not an end times book. On the contrary, this writing addresses and explores the aftermath of the apocalypse, specifically the mortal survivor's life on the earth after the great tribulation and the second coming of Jesus Christ. And at the risk of sounding pretentious, I know of no published book that presents, in such vivid detail, what human survivors will witness.

The Scriptures are surprisingly explicit and abundant concerning the blessed (but small) population of human survivors scattered throughout the world who will be left behind to live during the thousand-year millennial reign of Jesus. These men and women will have missed the rapture of the church, managed to survive the Great Tribulation with all of its plagues, opening of seals, the sounding of intermittent trumpets while refusing to take the mark of the beast, but, moreover, have held onto a relatively respectable level of belief in Jesus Christ. These survivors (both Jew and Gentile) have not been judged (as far as their eternity is concerned) at this point, and will remain on the earth during Jesus' reign. Although there will not be any unbelievers remaining upon the earth after the great and terrible day of His return, there will be *non-receivers* of Jesus' lordship. You will find, ironically, that many of these mortal survivors will, in time, actually refuse to recognize the authority of Jesus Christ and rebel against His Kingdom. Consequently, they will be duly and immediately punished on judgment day.

I am persuaded that many of these survivors will consider themselves Christians. They will be church goers or members who miss the rapture and be left behind upon the earth because of their lack of relationship with Him. Arguably, fifty percent of the church will be left behind according to Scripture. As a few examples: Two will be grinding at the mill – one shall be taken and the other left. Two shall be found in a field – one shall be taken and the other one is left. Two will be found in a bed – one shall be taken and the other left (Luke 17:34-36). Ten virgins with lamps – five will be taken and the other five left behind (Matthew 25:1-13). Do you see that the separation is consistently half of each group or couple?

You might find a fifty percent retention rate for the rapture a bit harsh, but I direct you to a Scripture that shows us that a person who says he is a Christian, or even a minister, may not be one at all. Matthew 7:21-23 tells of Jesus casting away men and women claiming to be Christians who casted out demons, prophesied in His name, and even performed many wonderful works for the Kingdom of God. But Jesus says to depart from Him, that they are workers of iniquity and that He never knew them, or in other words–He never had a relationship with them.

I would also suggest in this book that the Jewish people who are chosen to remain behind might very well be a population that will be considered believers once they see Him descending to the earth at His second coming. They will be Jews who are not wicked or evil, and have been chosen to remain on the earth because of the good life they lived and their quick acceptance of the King of kings.

Matthew 7:13-14 makes clear that most will enter into the wide gate of destruction rather than the narrow gate that leads to life eternal. And many of these people may profess some level of religion, or even some form of Christianity. But just like in the days of Noah, the wrath of God can wipe out an entire earth of humans and only leave behind eight souls–all of the same family. Many of those who will choose the wide door of eternal damnation will have been non-believers, for they will not merit any mercy at His coming. It is those who have some redeemable level of belief that may find the mercy needed to stay on the earth. Though they will miss the rapture, they also will be spared from hell and the lake of fire. At the end of the thousand years, these will be finally judged according to their belief in Jesus Christ and the life they lived while on the earth during the millennial reign.

Regretfully, I must concede that my ministry, creeping up on thirty-eight years now, has provided very limited teachings beyond what happens during the rapture. However, I personally know no other pastor or minister who teaches very much about the world and the earth's inhabitants after the second coming. I plan to rectify this shortcoming of mine with this book and a series of teachings I have constructed for congregations that will listen to me.

The church deserves the details surrounding the coming Kingdom of God. After all, Jesus said that teaching of the coming Kingdom of God (the Millennium) is the *reason* He was sent here in the first place (Luke 4:43). Also, He said to pray, *Thy Kingdom come, Thy will be done, on earth as it is in Heaven.* Jesus spent very little time alluding to the rapture and spent most of His time teaching on the coming one-thousand-year kingdom.

Truthfully, my research on this subject has changed my life. Like many ministers and students of the Gospel, I have taught the typical descriptions of life on earth during the thousand-year reign, such as: the lion will sleep with the lamb, there will be no wars, weapons will be made into farming equipment, human aging will not be an issue, Satan is cast into a bottomless pit (the abyss), the Antichrist and false prophet are cast into the Lake of Fire, there will be no repossessions of homes and properties, and that Satan is released for a short season to bring the final war against Christ and His rule on the earth. That pretty much sums up the range of the typical ministerial millennial instruction. I had previously dismissed teaching much of the Kingdom coming because I assumed there was very little scriptural reference available to research. How terribly wrong I have been. And respectfully, I have noticed some ministers who provide "kingdom keys" sermons who really need to review the Scriptures to ensure their accuracy.

I invite you to come on this journey with me, which is a quest for the important details of the coming Kingdom, which the apostles, prophets, and Jesus Christ have pointed to and guided us through; they have left a trail of breadcrumbs for us to follow.

Please read these following seven qualifiers; they will help you understand this unique book

1.) Allow me make mention in advance that I insist throughout this book that the *rapture and second coming of Jesus Christ is not the end of the world.* As you will read in chapter 1, there will be humans who will remain and survive, and who will serve Jesus Christ during His reign. And though very few will survive the terrible day of the Lord, there will be an accelerated repopulation of the world during this millennial period. These will be the people Jesus will reign over along with the immortal saints who were raptured and returned with Him. The surviving and growing population will make a choice to follow Jesus Christ or rebel against His kingship. Regretfully, many will deny and even oppose His kingdom on earth.

2.) Allow me to also mention that as you read the selected Scriptures throughout this book, you will notice two phrases: *The kingdom of God,* and *the kingdom of Heaven.* So as to avoid any confusion, *there is no difference between these two phrases, for they are interchangeable.* I base this conclusion from many commentaries that find no difference when forming parallels between the synoptic gospels (Matthew, Mark, and Luke). The two phrases in the New Testament are mentioned sixty-eight times. All thirty-two times that *the kingdom of God* is mentioned is found only in the book of Matthew. Matthew was reaching out to the Jewish people while writing his gospel. Therefore, the term *kingdom of God* was more acceptable to them, for they associated the kingdom of God with the millennial reign of the Messiah.

3.) For the sake of continuity, *I have assumed the premillennial rapture position,* which believes that Jesus Christ resurrects (raptures) all of the children of God, both dead and living, before the great and terrible day of the Lord. I write that these raptured people will be escorted to a judgment throne (BEMA) in order to receive their rewards, crowns, thrones, stars, and white robes. Many will have been rewarded for the good things they have done on earth, and others will find that their perceived good works were burnt away because of the lack of quality. These works can be compared to being as silver and gold, or wood, straw, stubble, and hay. There is a record of all good works that are marked for blessings, such as: good deeds to the widow and orphan, attention given to the poor and needy, allowances given to the feeble, visits made to the sick and imprisoned, preaching and teaching the word of God, and so on. Enoch recounts how God will remember those that were faithful to Him and reward them with great blessings of honor in His kingdom.

"And all the blessings destined for them I have recounted in the books. And He has assigned them their recompense, because they have been found to be such as loved heaven more than their life in the world, and though they were trodden under foot of wicked men, and experienced abuse and reviling from them and were put to shame, yet they blessed Me. And now I will summon the spirits of good who belong to the generation of light, and I will transform those who were born in darkness, who in the flesh were not recompensed with such honor as their faithfulness deserved. And I will bring forth in shining light those who have loved My holy Name, and I will seat each on the throne of his honor." (Enoch 108:10-12)

After this BEMA judgment, the raptured people will be escorted to the marriage supper of the Lamb. After this supper, the raptured saints will accompany Jesus Christ in His second coming to earth. They are described as the armies of Heaven (with the angels) invading the earth in order to destroy the works of wickedness and evil. The raptured saints shall remain on the earth with Jesus to reign with Him over all of the surviving humans for one thousand years. I believe that during the Great Tribulation, the martyrs (see Revelation 6:9-11) will join the other previously raptured saints in heaven (the second resurrection) as they are intermittently killed by the Antichrist. This is the second resurrection which John the revelator was referring to. But those who remain dead will remain in that state until after the millennial reign is completed. After the thousand years are over, the dead will be brought to the White Throne judgment and then cast into the lake of fire, which John refers to as *the second death*.

4.) Those who are raptured will be profoundly close in relationship with Jesus Christ and have proven themselves to be called some of the following descriptions: overcomers, victorious, profitable servants, those who are watching and waiting, those who did not faint, they endured testing and did not deny the faith, and whose garments were not soiled by a life of sin. *By no means am I suggesting that our works saves us, but there is a clear difference between those who are taken up in the rapture and those survivors left behind on the earth to serve Jesus as mortals.* Malachi refers to a book or scroll of remembrance, which is a registry of names God has marked as those who have merited escape from the great and terrible day of His wrath.

> Then those who feared the Lord talked with each other, and the Lord listened and heard. **A scroll of remembrance** was written in His presence concerning those who feared the Lord and honored His name. They will be mine, says the Lord Almighty, in the day when I make up my treasured possession. I will spare them, just as in compassion a man spares his son who serves him. **And you will again see the distinction between righteousness and the wicked, between those who serve God and those who do not** (Malachi 3:16-17, NIV).

5.) You will discover that I am not writing as a post-tribulation rapture believer, the position that teaches that the saints will be forced to endure the wrath of God upon the earth. This is an important qualifier, because this book is built upon the foundation that raptured saints escape the wrath of God, which to many students of eschatology account for the last three years of a seven-year tribulation. It is my opinion that the saints of God will not endure the wrath of God, but will to be given salvation (escape) from it. (1 Thessalonians 5:9)

Many of the Thessalonian believers feared that the rapture had taken place without them, for there were false teachers among them that were teaching such (as there are even to this day teaching that the rapture has already happened or there will be no rapture). But Paul gave the church (2 Thessalonians 2:1-10) three events to watch for that must take place prior to the rapture: (1) The lawless one will be revealed, (2) and a great apostasy will take place, (3) and the one who restrains will be removed.

To expound a bit on these three rapture prerequisites, first, the lawless one is the Antichrist who will be revealed to the church before it is raptured. To date, this has not happened. I realize that the Preterist and Historicist doctrines believe that this has already happened, however this book does not build off of this belief.

Second, though there have been many apostasies (Dark Ages, etc.), there is a coming apostasy that is forming right now in the world that is filled with such great deception that those deceived will believe they are still in the church. I am speaking of the worldwide organization of religions that are being formed aggressively by the Vatican that minimizes Jesus Christ but invites literally every ungodly belief (Wiccan, Muslim, Buddhism, Taoism, Hindu, and so on), all for the sake of unity and world peace. This worldwide religious organization will consider any church that refuses to be part of this world church a separatist, a hater of peace and tranquility. This church will be opposed and persecuted. This will be the greatest of all worldwide apostasies because it appeals to the humanist, agnostic, atheist, and most certainly the politically correct. I predict that evangelicals will be considered spiritual terrorists that must be stopped.

And third, when Paul refers to "...The one who now holds back will continue to do so till he is out of the way" (2 Thessalonians 2:7 NIV), he is saying that there is a person who is positioned by God to keep the Antichrist at bay. He will be divinely removed to allow the lawless one to wreak havoc throughout the world. starting with Israel. Commentaries battle over who is the one that is restraining the Antichrist. Because once he is removed, the rapture will take place. I am persuaded that the archangel Michael is the restrainer; and I am certainly among the majority believing he is so. Michael is the archangel over Israel, more specifically Jerusalem (Daniel 12:1). Michael is the prince and guardian angel of the Jews in Israel, and He is keeping (restraining) the anti-Christ from practicing his powers of darkness and seeking to promote Satan. Some commentaries believe the restrainer is the Holy Spirit, or the Bible, or the

Jewish State, or human government such as the United Nations, but most lean toward Michael as the one who restrains.

6.) It is also necessary for me to stipulate that because there is a constant opportunity for mankind to call upon the power of its free will—to choose Jesus Christ or not—I cannot in good conscience believe in a Calvinistic belief in which each individual has been predestined to go to hell or heaven, in light of the biblical evidence that there will be a second opportunity for a person who has missed the rapture, which can vindicate him during the millennium. As I mention in this book several times, the rapture event is not the end of the world as we know it. The rapture for many is not a heaven or hell moment. On the contrary, a man can live his life, miss the rapture, refuse the mark of the beast, survive the second coming, refuse to recant Jesus Christ (all of which are choices), and then, with his free will, choose to live for Christ for a thousand years in order to spend eternity in heaven.

7.) Throughout this book, I freely use the extra-biblical books of Enoch and 2 Baruch as supportive material. Please see Appendix A for the historical precedent and other validating reasons to include them.

CHAPTER ONE

The Return of Jesus Christ will be Terrifying

"People will faint from terror, apprehensive of what is coming to the world, for the heavenly bodies will be shaken."

(Luke 21:26 NIV)

In this chapter, I want to share with you a startling revelation—that being the tremendous amount of Scripture given to the *details* of Jesus Christ's return to earth at His second coming and the destruction He will bring with Him when He arrives. I have been crying out in my prayers for the Lord to come quickly so that my loved ones and I can enjoy the promised rapture, be removed from the results of God's wrath, and return as part of the establishment of Jesus' thousand-year-reign on earth (Revelation 22:20). For me personally, however, the tremendous amount of killing that will commence upon His return to earth never cognitively registered until now. Like you, I knew that the wicked were going to be punished, but the details and the magnitude of this carnage became far more disturbing than I imagined it would be for me. During my research, when I read how the literal hundreds of millions—probably billions—of angels are preparing and commissioned to kill billions of evil and wicked people, my compassion for these people rose up. I do realize that all of these evil people certainly deserve all the punishment coming to them, but at particular moments while writing this chapter, the research disturbed me so much that it affected my daily routines. Some of my family members suggested that I stop writing, but I knew I couldn't–if not for the sake of those who need to read it, then at least for myself and my ministry.

REMOVING THE WICKED WILL REQUIRE A RADICALLY DIVINE EVENT

I do not like evil or wicked people any more than the average person. Like you, I would like to see all of those hateful and demonic people gone. As acceptable as that statement probably is to you, we both know that evil and wickedness aren't going anyplace through our efforts. The government, the police, the military, our social workers, and even the Church's influence will not remove evil from us. We can certainly oppose evil, but nothing we have at our disposal can purge this earth from those who are intent on hurting and killing others. It's going to take a radical event to cleanse this world of the wicked, because Satan actually has an incredible foothold of authority on this earth. And the reason Satan has this authority on earth is because God gave it to him to fulfill His purposes.

Presently, Satan is ruling on this earth—not Jesus, not any powerful first-world nation, and certainly not the Church. Jesus told Pilate, *"…My kingdom is not of this world. If it were, my servants would fight to prevent my arrest by the Jewish leaders. But now my kingdom is from another place"* (John 18:36 NIV).

Luke actually goes further and details the conversation between Jesus and Satan, in which Satan blatantly states that all authority has been given to him as well as all the nations of the world. And his rule of all these kingdoms are his to give to anyone he desires to give them to (Luke 4:5-6). Paul is clear when he refers to Satan as the god of this age who has blinded all of the unbelievers throughout this world in which we live and breathe (2 Corinthians 4:4). Paul addresses the Ephesians and reminds them that, *"Wherein in time past ye walked according to the course of this world, according to the prince and power of the air, the spirit that now worketh in the children of disobedience"* (Ephesians 2:2 KJV).

It is no wonder to you or I that the world is full of sin and all nations are at odds with Jesus Christ. At some level, every nation is being influenced by the evil and darkness of Satan—covertly or otherwise. Paul tells the Romans that all of mankind is experiencing uninvited spiritual frustration of existing evil and vanity (Romans 8:20). Evil is essentially present—not by the choice of man, but rather subjected to it, as if mankind is subject to the leadership of evil.

In order to rid the world of all of this wickedness, it is going to take an all-out invasion of the earth to conquer Satan. Since the world is not yet under the rule of Jesus Christ, He is coming to simply (but violently) take over every nation and destroy all evil, whether the enemy is human or spirit. It is going to take a massive and radical event, as I previously mentioned, to purge this earth of the wicked, the demonic, of Satan himself, and all of people who are hopelessly evil. At the second coming of Christ, Satan will be cast into an abyss, and the false prophet and Antichrist will be thrown into the lake of fire. The influence of the wicked people of the world will also be destroyed on that great and terrible day of the Lord (Joel 2:31), and they will be cast into hell to await the great white throne judgment. Their wait in hell will be a thousand years of earth time.

Enter Jesus Christ

The Bible mentions the second coming of Jesus Christ many times and describes this horrific day as "terrible" at least seventy-nine times. The entire earth and air will be purged of all wickedness and evil, and only the Son of God can accomplish this feat. If you are a survivor of the second coming, you will immediately witness that Jesus' return will purge evil-doing humans through an outright blitz by the angels. Make no mistake, Jesus' initial intent upon His return is to kill. To utterly kill in such a ferocious manner that even the description of Jesus Christ's personage as He arrives is frightful.

John, the writer of Revelation, lays out a unique description of Jesus Christ: *"His head and his hairs were white like wool, as white as snow, and **His eyes were a flame of fire;** And His feet like unto fine brass, as if they burned in a furnace; and His voice was like the sound of many waters"* (Revelation 1:14-15 KJV). In Revelation 19, the terrifying description of His Second Coming continues. *"With justice he judges and makes war. **His eyes are like blazing fire**, and on His head are many crowns. ... **He is dressed in a robe dipped in blood** ..."* (Revelation 19:11-13 NIV). The description picks up and states, *"Out of His mouth comes **a sharp sword with which He strikes the nations**. He will rule them with **an iron scepter**. He treads the winepress of **the fury of the wrath of God Almighty"** (Revelation 19:15 NIV).

Are you catching these fearsome phrases by John? This is certainly not the same presentation or personality that the Son of God displayed during His earthly ministry.

The fierce depiction of Jesus at His return is not even a close rendering of the face of Jesus while He walked the earth, as described by Paul to the Philippians, *"But made Himself of no reputation, and took upon Himself the form of a servant, and was made in the likeness of men, and being found in appearance as a man, He humbled Himself, and became obedient unto death, even the death of the cross"* (Philippians 2:7-8 KJV). Nor does the depiction of Jesus Christ by Isaiah provide any relationship to the fierceness of John's Revelation description. *"...He had no beauty or majesty to attract us to Him, nothing in His appearance that we should desire Him"* (Isaiah 53:2 NIV). And notice how, after the resurrection, no one who was close to Jesus even recognized Him, because of the wondrous and beautiful, glorified body He had assumed (Luke 24:16). His newly acquired, resurrected, glorified body was a far cry from His former body that had no outstanding characteristics. He must have been a very dignified and powerful presence after His resurrection.

Getting back to John's fearsome description of Jesus— the comparisons of Jesus when He was on the earth to how He will look in the second coming are startling. His appearance from head to toe defies the human concept of a humble, loving, compassionate, and merciful man. This is because His intentions at the second coming are clearly seen to declare Himself as the King of Kings and the Lord of Lords, and to destroy everything that is high and lofty, evil and wicked.

You will discover, as I continually reiterate, that He comes to kill the wicked, evil and iniquitous people throughout the entire world—not just those in the nations surrounding Israel at the battle of Armageddon, or strictly the Middle Eastern countries. On the contrary, Jesus' attack will be worldwide, and His killings will be assisted by the innumerable angels who return with Him. *"The Son of Man will send out His angels, and they will weed out of His kingdom everything that causes sin all who do evil. They will throw them into the fiery furnace, where there will be weeping and gnashing of teeth. Then the righteous will shine like the sun in the kingdom of their Father. He who has ears let him hear"* (Matthew 13:41-43 NIV). Can you just imagine this scene in your mind, with several hundred million angels, per se, pouring out of the skies, maybe so dense as to blot out the sun, with the intent to kill and destroy the sinful and non-believing populations?

The moment of His arrival is going to be so incredible— heralded by the sounds of millions of powerful, angelic wings, the piercing blasts of angelic trumpets of His coming, the shrilling screams of terror from those who have no hope, and with the face of Him who all the inhabitants of the earth will flee from. Previously, when I thought and prayed about the second coming and the rapture, I specifically concentrated on the euphoria of the experience we will all have as we are caught up to meet Jesus in the clouds. I really didn't think much about the carnage His return would cause. I didn't know about the plethora of details concerning the perishing of the evil and wicked remaining on the earth.

THE DEATH ANGELS AND THEIR KILLING INSTRUMENTS

For instance, Enoch actually mentions the death angels that are preparing special killing instruments for the great and terrible day of the Lord. And there are special instruments of killing for the sinners of the earth and specific instruments being forged by the angels to destroy the fallen angels on the earth as well. *"Yet the sinners shall be destroyed before the face of the Lord of Spirits, and they shall be banished off the face of His earth, and they shall perish forever and ever. For I saw all the angels of punishment abiding there and preparing all the instruments of Satan. And I asked the angel of peace who went with me: For whom are they preparing these instruments? And he said unto me: They are prepared for the kings and the mighty of the earth, that they may thereby be destroyed"* (Enoch 53:2-5).

I mentioned that I had a hard time writing these words about the terrible day of the second coming, but Enoch had an especially difficult time witnessing these horrendous events. You will notice that the writer, Enoch, describes the second coming of Jesus as unbearable for him to watch, even in a vision. *"I saw how a mighty quaking made the heaven of heavens to quake, and the host of the Most High, and the angels, a thousand thousands and ten thousand times ten thousand, were disquieted with a great disquiet. And the Head of Days sat on the throne of His glory, and* *angels and the righteous stood around Him. **And a great trembling seized me, and fear took hold of me, and my loins gave way, and dissolved were my reins, and I fell upon my face.** And Michael sent another angel from among the holy ones and He raised me up my spirit returned; **for I had not been able to endure the look of this host, and the commotion and the quaking of the heaven"** (Enoch 60:1-3). Malachi 3:2-4 also provides the reader with sobering descriptions of the return of Jesus Christ that are astounding.

Who are these people who the angels are sent to destroy? It is important to define who these wicked, evil, and unbelieving are; (and we will define them more fully). They are those who opposed Jesus Christ and His Church, those who opposed Israel, and those who persecuted and martyred His people. Jesus Christ will have an archangel cast Satan into the abyss, and kill the Antichrist and the false prophet by casting them into the lake of fire. Jesus then will declare total victory over the earth. All of this carnage will be completed within one day, the Great and Terrible Day of the Lord (Joel 2:31).

The prophet Jude writes a very short but determined New Testament book defining those who are wicked and evil. Jude uses cutting words that describe those who reach the point of such ungodliness that no hope of salvation is left for them. *"These men are blemishes at your love feasts, eating with you without the slightest qualm – shepherds that feed only themselves. They are clouds without rain, blown along by the wind; autumn trees, without fruit and uprooted – twice dead. They are wild waves of the sea, foaming up their shame; wandering stars, for whom the blackest darkness has been reserved forever. Enoch, the seventh from Adam, prophesied about these men: See the Lord is coming with thousands upon thousands of His holy ones to judge everyone, and to convict all the ungodly of all the ungodly acts they have done in the ungodly way, and of the harsh words ungodly sinners have spoken against Him.*

These men are grumblers and faultfinders; they follow their own evil desires; they boast about themselves and flatter others for their own advantage" (Jude 12-16 NIV).

Though Jesus could destroy all of the wicked and the unbelievers upon the earth by just the burst of His nostrils, He has chosen to send out His angels to separate the good from the bad, which can only be done divinely. As humans, we have no ability to glean the fields of the tares and wheat, or sift the threshing floor of the chaff. This is an impossible mandate for man; for only God can righteously judge.

THE SECOND COMING OF JESUS CHRIST
IS NOT THE END OF THE WORLD-
THERE WILL BE SURVIVORS

The second coming of Jesus Christ, as horrific as it sounds, is not the end of the world. Many Christians believe or have been taught that the rapture of the church is the end of the world, and that you will either end up, at that point, in heaven or in hell. This isn't true. Well, at least it isn't true for those who survive the Great Tribulation.

When Jesus returns to the earth, He will allow a small remnant of the human population to survive the great day of the Lord (some Jews and others Gentiles). The actual end of the world is when man experiences the white throne judgment of God and the earth and the heavens (atmosphere, sky, and the exosphere) are burnt with a fervent heat. This fire (that we will speak about in chapter four) is a fire that will literally burn the earth to the place of nonexistence. This, then, is actually the end of the world as we know it, but does not occur until after the thousand-year reign of Jesus Christ. So, once again, the rapture does not mark the end of the world, and neither does the second coming of Christ.

Some may say that it seems like God is giving the surviving humans a second chance. Since they didn't qualify for the rapture, and they survived the wrath of God upon the earth, why should they merit the favor of a further opportunity? It begs the questions then: Who are the humans who will not survive? And who are the humans who are chosen to survive?

The Jewish survivors will bask in the beauty of the renewed earth, and they will be called holy, *"In that day the Branch of the Lord will be beautiful and glorious, and the fruit of the land will be **the pride and glory of the survivors** in Israel. Those who are left in Zion, **who remain in Jerusalem, will be called holy, all who are recorded among the living in Jerusalem"** (Isaiah 4:2-3 NIV). God will return the pride and morale of the survivors, especially that of the Jews. The shame and guilt of their past sins will dissipate and the survivors will be enveloped with a new sense of hope and joy.

Once a person has been brought before the judgment throne of God, it is evidently too late to repent. All of us have that opportunity right now, during our entire life, to confess our belief in Christ, confess our sins, plead the blood of Jesus Christ, and call upon the cross of Calvary. After you die or stand in judgment, all of your opportunities are gone.

WHO ARE THE WICKED HUMANS WHO WILL NOT SURVIVE?

Who are these wicked ones? This question only God can answer—and then identify and separate them from the good people (Matthew 13:41-43). Sadly, many civilizations regard evil as relative—seeing bad as good and good as bad. This is the reason mankind cannot separate the tares from the wheat among us, or the sheep from the goats. Jesus Christ and the angels of heaven alone will be able to sift through the entire human race on that great and terrible day, and identify the evil among us.

The wicked, who exhausted God's mercy, are those who do not believe that Jesus Christ rose from the dead; they are atheists, agnostics, mockers of the Word, sinful blind creatures, idolatrous, practitioners of witchcraft, workers of iniquity, cruel and unmerciful, plotters and schemers of evil, pagans (multiple god worshippers), the violent who hunt the weak and feeble, those with immoral lives as fornicators or adulterers, unshameful scoundrels who lie in wait for blood, cultists, those of the spirit of antichrist, the malicious, murderers, the unrelenting transgressors of divine laws of God, the evil principled, those who set snares on the unsuspecting, those who live to cheat, steal and lie, and those who choose not to retain God in their minds. I suppose this list could go on for pages. But these are those humans who will not be able to repent at this point. It will be too late for them. Sadly, when they realize how terribly wrong they have been, there will be no more room to ask for a pardon or forgiveness.

Read how the prophet Baruch describes how it is too late for those who refused Jesus Christ when they could have had Him as their Lord. Baruch's writings are more poignant and detailed in explaining that there is no mercy or an opportunity for evil people to confess their sins in order to receive a little respite from their punishment. *"For behold, the Most High will cause all these things to come.* **There will not be an opportunity to repent anymore, nor a limit to the times, nor a duration of the periods, nor a chance to rest, nor an opportunity to pray, nor sending up petition, nor giving knowledge, nor giving love, nor opportunity of repentance, nor supplicating for offenses, nor prayers of the fathers, nor intercessions of the prophets, nor help of the righteous"** (2 Baruch 85:12-13). How absolutely frightening it is to imagine running out of time to repent or to ask God for forgiveness. The very idea that God can turn a deaf ear to those who are crying out is so very sad and hard for me to absorb.

Just as an interim encouragement to you: If you are finding yourself in this litany of sinfulness, please know that there is a difference between being a *wicked* person and being a *weak* person. There is a difference between living the life of a sinner and sinning occasionally. God knows those who have a good heart from those who have no conscience. This is why it's vital that God judges us and not man. And it is also comforting to know that Jesus' mercy extends to those who believe in Him as the only Son of God. These believers may very well be extended mercy to survive the second coming from the judgment because of their belief in Jesus. But as I said, I don't know; only God knows how to judge the quick and the dead. If you are not a believer in Jesus Christ, or worse, if you have denied, opposed, or rejected Jesus Christ, then I regretfully (but decisively) say that you will not be extended His mercy, because you are not one of His that He is returning for.

It is quite possible that many Americans may suffer great consequences, (as will those in other nations) and will experience a national catastrophe because of our country's sins. Entire nations could be completely destroyed. As you probably know all too well, the United States has removed the Ten Commandments from some of our federal buildings, removed prayer in our schools, Bibles are not permitted in many institutions (except prisons, ironically), evangelizing in the military is not permitted, homosexuality is becoming the norm, many cities do not allow the displaying of Christian expression, especially during the holidays, businesses are being sued who refuse to go against their religious beliefs (such as bakeries, florists, elected officials, and other businesses). Evangelicals have been compared with terrorists, television productions disallow the use of the name of Jesus on air, and prefers the universal and all-inclusive term "God" to be used instead. Political correctness has overtaken the truth, college sports chaplains are being removed, atheistic chaplains for the military are being employed, the United States Supreme Court has redefined marriage, and if a Christian speaks out against same-sex marriages, he or she can be cited for a hate crime or minimally, labeled a bigot. I fear for our nation's future when we consider the coming judgments of God at the second coming of Jesus Christ. I am not referring here to the judgments during the great tribulation period; for as I have said, this book is not an end times writing, but rather a post second-coming guide for those who survive it.

Some nations, for that matter, will be so sinful and blind that when Jesus and His army attack the wickedness of the earth, ironically some will attempt to attack Him! *"Then I saw the beast and the kings of the earth and their armies gather together* **to make war against the rider on the horse and His army***. But the beast was captured, and with him the false prophet …the two of them were thrown alive into the fiery lake of burning sulphur. The rest of them were killed with the sword that came out of the mouth of the rider on the horse, and all the birds gorged themselves on their flesh"* (Revelation 19:19-21 NIV). Jesus will utterly vanquish His attacking and retaliating enemies and any and all opposition that are squared off against His coming kingdom. The wicked will remain wicked and will become so devilishly angry with God and Jesus Christ that they will fight for their respective nationalistic and personal causes.

I would counsel you that if you witness the tribulation, do not side with those individuals or nations who oppose the God of Abraham, Isaac, and Jacob, who is the Father of the only Son, the Lord Jesus Christ, and who is followed by faithful Christians and messianic Jews (Judeo-Christian believers). No matter if the nation that you live in is unified against Christianity, no matter the level of deception, no matter how many worldwide are opposed to Christ—do not turn your back on Him. But trust that He will remember you during His second coming, for that will mark your eternal survival.

Why will certain nations be spared?

Not every nation on earth shall experience complete destruction; the nations that did not oppose or curse Israel or her people will actually escape the mass destruction by the King of Kings. Notice in 2 Baruch, that Jesus will summon all the nations of the earth for judgment based upon how they treated Israel and the Hebrews: *"This is the word. After the signs have come of which I have spoken to you before, when the nations are moved and the time of my Anointed One comes, He will call all nations,* **and some of them He will spare, and others He will kill. These things will befall the nations, which will be spared by Him. Every nation that has not known Israel and which has not trodden down the seed of Jacob will live. And this is because some from all nations have been subjected to your people"** (2 Baruch 72:2-5).

There will be some nations (especially their kings) that will plead for forgiveness and say that they now understand the evil they have committed. They will attempt to repent. They will attempt to confess their new-found belief and faith in God, but they will be rejected by God, **"In those days shall the mighty and the kings who possess the earth implore Him to grant them a little respite from His angels of punishment** *to whom they were delivered, that they might fall down and worship before the Lord of Spirits, and* **confess their sins before Him, We have now learnt that we should glorify and bless the Lord of kings and Him who is King over all kings** (Enoch 63:1,4). But their pleas will be to no avail, for they will be too late with their confessions, and His judgments come without respect of persons. *"And in the day of our suffering and* **tribulation He saves us not, and we find no respite for confession** *that our Lord is true in all His works, and in His judgments and His justice, and His judgments have no respect of persons"* (Enoch 63:8). It is grievous to read this, but remember that God's foundation is holiness, and all sin will have a reckoning day. For those who have the Savior Jesus Christ, He reckoned with our sins by His blood; for those who are not in Christ, they must reconcile their sins by themselves with a most torturous eternal death. He is the perfect judge, the exquisite righteousness, and He metes out incomprehensible judgments.

WILL ALL THE JEWS
SURVIVE OR BE SAVED?

There are questions that emerge as to whether all the Jews will be saved, survive, or be pardoned as a people, being that they are the physical, chosen people of God from the seed of Abraham, Isaac, and Jacob.

According to the book of Romans, most Jews were so antichrist in their beliefs that God has and will give them over to their hardened hearts. These are those who have alienated themselves from salvation by their words and their deeds. *"I do not want you to be ignorant of this mystery, brothers, so that you may not be conceited:* **Israel has experienced a hardening in part until the full number of the Gentiles has come in. And so all Israel shall be saved,** *as it is written: The deliverer will come out of Zion; He will turn godlessness away from Jacob. And this is My covenant with them when I take away their sins. As far as the Gospel is concerned,* **they are enemies on your account***; but as far as the election is concerned, they are loved on account of the patriarchs"* (Romans 11:25-28 NIV). And actually, the Jewish people have been oppositional to Jesus as the Messiah. In verse 25, there is a hardening of their hearts that happened to the Israelites toward the Gospel of Jesus Christ and to the Christians that follow the good news. This reflects the evident loss of many Jews who have rejected Jesus Christ. The hardening of their hearts is comparative to Romans chapter 1 in which God gives them over to a reprobate mind, or gives them up to their own hearts' desires. In verse 26 of Romans chapter 11, the phrase, *and all Israel shall be saved* is evidently speaking of the nation of Israel as a whole and not each individual Jew. God is saying that after the second coming, He will pardon the nation for their sins, He will bring restitution to their nation, and this is, of course, notwithstanding the judgment of His arrival. But each Jew is judged independent of his or her Hebrew heritage, just like the rest of us.

The writer of Romans draws a line between those who are genuine, authentic, practicing Jews and those who are non-religious Jewish men. Not every Jew that calls him or herself a Jew is actually an authentic, bona fide Jew. These egocentric Jews are irreligious and pretentious liars according to the apostle John. *"I will make those who are of the synagogue of Satan, who claim to be Jews though they are not, but liars. I will make them come and fall down at your feet and acknowledge that I have loved you"* (Revelation 3:9 NIV). These so-called Jews are non-worshippers of God. They are under the influence of Satan (*"of the synagogue of Satan"*), and are of the most wicked and carnal sort. Notice that these pseudo Jews, who historically have been opposed to Christians will bow down before them and acknowledge that God was with them all along, to their great grief and shame.

I must remain faithful to the Scriptures to answer the question "Will all Jews be saved?" by stating if they have rejected or denied Jesus Christ, then they will die in their sins like everyone else who rejects Him.

The Jews had tremendous opportunities afforded to them to believe in the Son of God. For instance, the entire gospel was preached *first to the Jews*, then to the Gentiles (Romans 1:16). The Jewish people have had their exceptional opportunities to accept Jesus Christ from Him personally for three and one half years while He walked the earth—all prior to any evangelism offered to the Gentiles. The Jews had ample time to receive salvation. Jesus was expressly sent to the house of Israel and not initially to the Gentiles (Matthew 15:24). But as the Gospels and history has shown, the Jews didn't receive Jesus Christ as the Messiah. *"He came unto His own, and His own received Him not"* (John 1:11 KJV). And, most fortunately for us who are Gentiles, His mercy consequently was extended to us *goyim*, unclean, pagans. Indeed, this became known as the time of the Gentiles. Once it was clear that the Hebrew people were not going to receive Jesus as the only Son of God and Savior of the world, God turned to the nations that did not know anything about the true God nor did they (the Gentiles) even seek Him. *"...I was found by those who did not seek Me; I revealed myself to those who did not ask for Me. But concerning Israel he says, all day long I have held out my hands to a disobedient and obstinate people"* (Romans 10:20-21 NIV).

Jesus paid the vast majority of His attention to Israel. Though there were small instances in which Jesus ministered to a Gentile or Samaritan, the lion's share of His concentration was to the house of Israel. Gentiles didn't receive direct efforts of conversion until chapter 10 of the book of Acts, where Peter the apostle was sent (and initially he was reluctant to do so) to Cornelius' house (Italian Gentiles) to preach the gospel. They were actually the first Gentiles to receive the word of God and to receive the Holy Spirit, as recorded in the Word of God. The Hebrews were extremely aggressive against the converting Christians. The Sanhedrin sent out men throughout Israel to kill any Jew that converted to Christianity. Actually one of these men was Saul, who later became known as the apostle Paul.

Today, however, in the twenty-first century, many Jews are turning from their ancient religion and converting into paganism or not believing in God at all; they are not true Jews. According to the *Jewish Weekly*, June 24, 2009 issue, Steve Lipmann stated that the once male-heavy attendance at Jewish synagogue services, as well as volunteer services, have largely disappeared. Rabbi Jeffrey K. Salkin, rabbi of Temple Beth Am in Bayonne, New Jersey, and author of many books reports, "It is unfortunate that men are increasingly distancing themselves from Jewish life as worshippers, as students of the Torah, and as synagogue leaders." Steve Byme, director of the American Jewish Committee Department of Contemporary Jewish Life, regretfully proclaims that this exodus of men from practicing Judaism has become so extreme that it may have become irreversible. "The question is not whether or not the pendulum has swung too far, but that men are disappearing from the synagogue." These Jews, who do not believe in God, will need to face the judgment throne of God for abandoning the God of Abraham, Isaac, and Jacob.

My best deduction is that the Jewish people will have their day in judgment just like all the nations of the world. However, the Scriptures are quite clear that the surviving Jews will be given special treatment and attention during the millennial reign, but not before facing the consequences as a nation on that great and terrible day of the Lord.

As a final, and exceptional opportunity, the Lord will afford the Jews a great season of evangelism in Israel in order to convert as many of the house of Israel as He can prior to the second coming. He will send out the two witnesses to preach for three-plus years with great power and miracles, and He will also send out an army of elected Jewish evangelists. He will specially seal selected Jews, some 144,000 of them, and will set them aside to share the gospel with the Israelites (Revelation 7:9-10) during the great tribulation. They will number 12,000 sealed men of God for each of the original twelve tribes. They will be comparable to 144,000 Apostle Pauls propagating the Word of God and converting Israel to a national repentance. It will be an unprecedented attempt by God to turn His people back to Him.

The question as to how many Jews in Israel will survive the second coming is actually addressed by Zechariah, as you will see below. Many believe that God will protect the land of Israel from another invasion or destruction, but this isn't true. Actually, the coming destruction of Israel will be terrible. Your study of Israeli history teaches you that Israel has had more than her lion's share of invasions, occupations, exiles, and destructions, but none will compare to what is going to happen during Jesus' invasion.

You will witness that one-third of the population of Jews in Israel will survive the Battle of Armageddon, the destructive second coming of Jesus Christ; with two-thirds of the Jews being destroyed. Take a look at Zechariah's breakdown of the Jewish people during the great and terrible day of the Lord: "*In the whole land, declares the Lord, **two-thirds will be struck down and perish; yet one-third will be left in it. This third I will bring in the fire**; I will refine them like silver and test them like gold. They will call on my name and I will answer them; I will say, they are my people, they will say, the Lord is my God. A day of the Lord is coming when your plunder will be divided among you. I will gather the nations to Jerusalem to fight against it; the city will be captured, the houses ransacked, and the women raped. Half of the city will go into exile, but the rest of the people will not be taken from the city. Then the Lord will go out against those nations, as He fights in the day of battle. On that day his feet will stand on the Mount of Olives, east Jerusalem, and the Mount of Olives will be split in two from east to west...you will flee as you fled from an earthquake*" (Zechariah 13:8-9, 14:1-4, 5 NIV). So clearly, not all the Jews will be saved solely based upon their naturalized Hebrew roots; the Jews must receive Christ. I will admit that once the Jews see Jesus coming out of the skies to avenge His Kingdom, they apparently will have a revelation of His identity as the Son of God, the Messiah, and immediately become believers. This does beg the question in my heart, will there be converted Jews at the very moment they see Him coming out of the clouds?

And if the destruction and carnage is not enough, there will be mass hysteria among the surviving Jews, once they see that the Son of God is truly the rejected Jesus Christ whom they have persecuted in times past as a people, *"And I will pour out on the house of David and the inhabitants of Jerusalem a spirit of grace and supplication.* ***They will look upon me, the one they have pierced, and they will mourn for Him as one mourns for an only child, and grieve bitterly for Him as one grieves for a firstborn son. On that day the weeping in Jerusalem will be great"*** (Zechariah 12:10-11 NIV). This is the first and only mention of grace offered to any inhabitants of the earth at His second coming. And all of the tribes and clans of Israel will bitterly and regretfully wail for their spiritual blindness, the hardening of their hearts, and also for what they have done to Jesus at His crucifixion. However, there is a redeeming hope from Isaiah to the Jews in which he says, *"The Redeemer will come to Zion, to those in Jacob, who repent of their sins, declares the Lord"* (Isaiah 59:20 KJV).

To balance this chapter properly, I want to share with you how wonderful the raptured people will be blessed, gifted, and yes, empowered. The glory of the resurrected saints of God is beyond words, and somehow I have been able to describe to some degree the level of immortality His beloved children will experience. The books of Enoch and Baruch, along with the canonized books of the Bible, have helped me with more colorful, wondrous words and phrases that better depict those who will be blessed upon the earth during His reign. The survivors (though far different than the raptured population) will incur enormous blessings as well. The survivors' life on earth will be very much like what Adam and Eve experienced in the Garden of Eden along with all the benefits of seeing the Savior on a daily basis for a blessed one thousand years.

WHO ARE THE RESURRECTED (RAPTURED) PEOPLE?

The raptured people are those who will be called up to the clouds in a mass "catching away" to meet Jesus in the air, taken to heaven and their bodies made glorious and immortal. They are a completely separate being from the humans who survive and remain upon the earth, for those will still be mortal beings.

These children of God are true followers of Christ, both alive and dead, that are raised up, (raptured or resurrected) and taken from the earth. *"Behold, I tell you a mystery;* **we will not all sleep,** *but we will be changed, in a moment, in the twinkling od an eye, at the last trumpet; for the trumpet shall sound,* **and the dead will be raised imperishable,** *and we will all be changed"* (1 Corinthians 15:51-52 KJV). Paul also comforts the Thessalonian church with the revelation of the rapture as well, *"For the Lord Himself will come down from heaven, and with a loud command, with the voice of the archangel and with the trumpet of God,* **and the dead in Christ will rise first. After that, we who are still alive and are left will be caught up together with them in the clouds to meet the Lord in the air.** *And so we will be with the Lord forever. Therefore encourage each other with these words"* (1Thessalonians 4:16-18 NIV). The time required for this to happen will be just a moment—that is, in a twinkling of an eye. The first trumpet will be for the dead to arise, and the second and last trumpet will be for the living to be changed into immortality and to be caught up to meet the Lord in the air.

These raptured beings will escape all of the horrible events during the latter part of the tribulation, which is called the wrath of God. (Some believe the wrath of God to be the last three and one half years of a seven-year great tribulation. Others believe it to be a shorter time nearer to the end of the seven-year period). Following the outpouring of God's wrath, the raptured beings will return with Christ at His second coming in order to reign with Him during the millennium. In actuality, if you are reading this book prior to the second coming, then you will really benefit far better if you were to choose to accept Christ's salvation now and become one of the resurrected or raptured ones. If you do, you will avoid all of the horrible events that occur during the wrath of God and at the return of Jesus Christ. You will be spared all of the terrifying judgments of God, once the saving blood of Jesus Christ has covered you.

As a survivor, you will notice a very special beauty about these risen, immortal people who will reign with King Jesus. These resurrected, spiritual beings, will have glorified bodies much like Jesus Christ, and have miraculous abilities, as Baruch noted: *"**Miracles**, however, will appear in their own time to those who are saved because of their works...For they shall see that world which is now invisible to them, and they will see a time which is now hidden to them. And time will no longer make them older. **For they will live in the heights of that world and they will be like the angels and be equal to the stars. And they will be changed into any shape, which they wished, from beauty to loveliness, and from light to the splendor of glory.** For the extents of Paradise will be spread out for them, **and to them will be shown the beauty of the majesty of the living beings under the throne**, as well as all the hosts of the angels, those who are held by my word now lest they show themselves, **...until their coming has arrived"** (2 Baruch 51:7-12). A fair question could be, why are these people so different from those remaining on the earth as survivors? The main difference would be that these risen souls hate this world and everything that is in it—that which tempts, titillates, or promises grandeur outside of God. The prophet Enoch says it so well: *"For He has preserved the lot of the righteous; **because they have hated and despised this world of unrighteousness, and have hated all its works and ways** in the name of the Lord of Spirits: for in His name are they saved..."* (Enoch 48:7).

If you are interested in becoming one of these raptured individuals, then I would implore you to repent of your sins, be baptized in the name of Jesus Christ, receive the Holy Spirit, and detest this present world.

THE JUDGMENT WILL BE WORLDWIDE, TOUCHING EVERY NATION

No doubt billions from every corner of the earth will die. The fear of God's avenging will be overwhelming for all of the wicked. They will try to run and hide from Jesus when they see Him coming out of the clouds with His army of angels and His bride in tow. Sadly, they will find no place to hide from the wrath of God, *"Men will flee to caves in the rocks and to holes in the ground from the dread of the Lord and the splendor of His majesty, when He rises and shakes the earth. In that day men will throw away rodents and bats their idols of silver and idols of gold, which they made to worship. They will flee to caverns in the rocks and to the overhanging crags from the dread of the Lord and the splendor of His majesty, when He rises to shake up the earth"* (Isaiah 2:19-21 NIV). Here John the Revelator describes what Isaiah also saw of the overwhelming fear of all the inhabitants of the earth and their attempt to hide and flee from the terrifying King of Kings. *"The sky receded like a scroll, rolling up, and every mountain and island was removed from its place. **The kings of the earth, the princes, the generals, the rich, the mighty, and every slave and every free man hid in caves and the rocks of the mountains. They called to the mountains and the rocks, 'Fall on hide and us** from the face of Him that sits on the throne and from the wrath of the Lamb! For the great day of their wrath has come, and who can stand?"* (Revelation 6:14-17 ESV). How does one hide or run from God? Where can you go, what cave can conceal you from the eyes of the returning Savior? There is no place on earth, under the earth, or in the sea can one find a place to flee from God Almighty. But many will attempt to.

WORLD LEADERS AND THE RICH WILL TRY TO HIDE THEMSELVES

When I read these Scriptures on how the kings and presidents of all nations will flee and hide in the mountains and rocks it reminds me of the many secret bunkers, just in the United

States alone, that are available for our leaders and the wealthy in case of a doomsday scenario. There are several of these emergency command posts that are entrenched deep into the mountains of Pennsylvania, Colorado, Virginia, and West Virginia. Likewise, I would assume that many nations have a protocol to escort their leaders into similar command center retreats, like America's NORAD in the Cheyenne Mountain Complex in Colorado Springs, Colorado. These bunkers boast of the capability to withstand a direct nuclear hit and still retain survivors. Not so when Jesus comes with the wrath of God. No mountain can hide them or protect them. Many wealthy people have built everything from basic to elaborate family bunkers, and even extremely wealthy community bunkers for the preparation of an end time survival. Some wealthy men across the world have built end times bunkers that can sustain a small community for those who can afford to live in these exotic, but fortified facilities for long periods of time. These underground bunkers are well stocked with food and supplies to last quite a while—in some cases years. But there is no place to hide from the face of Jesus Christ. Ironically, many men will pray that the mountains will fall upon them in order to hide from the coming judgments of God. You can almost imagine the terror that will also be shared with the fish of the oceans, the birds of the air, and beasts of the field; all life will tremble at His arrival. *"The fish of the sea, the birds in the sky, the beasts of the field, every creature that moves along the ground, and all the people on the face of the earth will tremble at my presence"* (Ezekiel 38:20 NIV).

To add to the trembling and confusion of the earth, His arrival will be so terrifying that, strangely, we won't experience either day or night. The sky will be filled with the presence of God as evidenced by lightning, black smoke of the Shekinah, such as appeared on Mount Sinai when Moses received the Ten Commandments, hundreds of millions of fiery brilliant angels descending upon the earth, and the incredible presence of the Mighty Son of God's armies, all of which will affect the weather, the sunlight and moon, and even the time of day. Actually, no one has ever seen a day like this before, in that the atmosphere will be so divinely complex that you cannot call it day time or night time, for it will be neither. Take a look at this very interesting observation of Zechariah: *"And it shall come to pass in that day, that **the light shall not be clear, nor dark: But it shall be one day which shall be known to the Lord, not day, nor night: but it shall come to pass, that at evening time it shall be light"* (Zechariah 14:6-7 KJV).

When John the Revelator wrote what he saw during the second coming, he was so afraid that he fell dead in the vision (Revelation 1:17). And like John, Isaiah, Ezekiel, Zechariah, and Jeremiah's description of this terrible day, it is quite clear that the carnage will involve the entire earth, not just the Middle East or those who fight in the Battle of Armageddon. Jeremiah was clear when he wrote that everyone throughout the earth would be affected. I don't mean to make this statement elementary, but in the Scripture below, you will notice I embolden five phrases that state emphatically that the judgment of God goes out to the whole earth—everywhere:

*"See, I am beginning to bring disaster on the city that bears my Name, and will you indeed go unpunished? You will not go unpunished, for I am calling down a sword **upon all that live on the earth**, declares the Lord Almighty. Now prophesy all these words against them and say to them: The Lord will roar from on high; he will thunder from his holy dwelling and roar mightily against his land. He will shout like those who tread the grapes, **shout against all who live on the earth**. The tumult will resound to the ends of the earth, for the Lord will bring charges against nations; **he will bring judgment on all mankind** and put the wicked to the sword, declares the Lord. This is what the Almighty says: Look! Disaster is spreading **from nation to nation;***

a mighty storm is rising from the ends of the earth. At that time those slain by the hand of the Lord will be **everywhere – from one end of the earth to the other.** They will not be mourned or gathered up or buried, but will be like refuse lying on the ground" (Jeremiah 25:29-33 NIV). Jeremiah really captures the absoluteness of the Lord and His rage worldwide. Jeremiah also relates to the reader that the attitude of the survivors is either total shock or total apathy, for they could not mourn or even have individual gravesites to weep over their deceased. Due to the enormous amount of worldwide deaths, it appears that the dead will require mass graves.

The wrath of God is not intended for His children

I certainly do not want to leave you with the notion that Jesus is only an angry King. On the contrary. He will be the consummate, loving King of Kings and Lord of Lords to the survivors. He will love and care for the survivors and will lovingly teach them God's laws of right and wrong. As for His raptured, immortal people, He will reign with them over all the earth, for He will share His throne and inheritance with them. *"The Lord will roar from Zion and thunder from Jerusalem; the earth and sky will tremble.* **But the Lord will be a refuge for His people"** (Joel 3:16-18 NIV). If you read Joel 2:23-28 (NIV), you might notice how God promises plentiful blessings and be the one *"who will work wonders for you."* The wrath of Jesus Christ will not be directed at the raptured saints of the living God, **"For God did not appoint us to suffer wrath** but to receive salvation through our Lord Jesus Christ" (1 Thessalonians 5:9 NIV). The Church, will see the second coming of Jesus Christ as a most joyful and wondrous celebration. His Church has been waiting, praying and watching for His return for at least two thousand years now. What the wicked and unbeliever will see as terrifying, His people will see as the uniting of a groom and bride. And it is His intention to give the entire earth and the kingdom of God to the raptured people. *"Fear not little flock, for it is your Father's good pleasure to give you the Kingdom"* (Luke 12:32 KJV).

As a matter of fact, He loves His children so much that the wicked will be removed from the earth for the raptured people's sake. God does not want to have the evil and wicked of this world standing in the presence of His resurrected children. *"And He will deliver them up to the angels for punishment, to execute vengeance on them because they have oppressed His children and His elect. And they shall be a spectacle for the righteous and for His elect: they shall rejoice over them, because the wrath of the Lord of Spirits resteth upon them, and His sword is drunk with their blood. And the righteous and the elect shall be saved that day, **and they shall never thenceforward see the face of the sinners and unrighteous.** And they shall have been clothed with garments of glory, and these shall be garments of life from the Lord of Spirits: and your garments shall not grow old, nor your glory pass away before the Lord of Spirits"* (Enoch 62:11-13, 16). The people of God will not have to be concerned about the wicked and evil people who may still be hiding out in the world, waiting to either persecute or kill them for their faith in God. Jesus ensures that there will not be a time, henceforth, that a raptured person will ever have to confront an accuser, a harasser, or a killer ever again.

Jesus has been preparing for His people to live with Him for all eternity since His ascension to Heaven. The raptured children of God will all have beautiful mansions built and waiting for them in Heaven where God Almighty resides. Enoch had a chance to peek at these mansions, *"And there I saw the mansions of the elect and the mansions of the holy..."* (Enoch 41:2). Jesus also referred to these magnificent houses built by God Himself, *"In my Father's house there are many mansions. If it were not so, I would have told you. I go to prepare a place for you"* (John 14:2 KJV). Some would have you to believe that these mansions are not literal. But I believe, based upon the Scriptures and commentary, that these houses in heaven are very much real. Among their beautiful homes and streets, the raptured people will also have, among many divine things, great and inexhaustible wisdom. *"And in that place I saw the fountain of righteousness which was inexhaustible: and around it were many fountains of wisdom; and all the thirsty drank of them, and were filled with wisdom"* (Enoch 48:1).

THERE WILL BE A MASSIVE CLEANUP PROGRAM BY THE HUMAN SURVIVORS

As a survivor, expect to see the remains of the carnage, destruction, the mountains of accumulated debris, and heaps of corpses beyond any of our imaginations. The amount of dead bodies littering the land of nations throughout the world will be so vast that the remaining survivors will forego funerals, wakes, and separate burial plots, in lieu of gathering the dead either for mass burial or mass cremation. Expect to be asked to assist in the massive cleanup. Here is what Ezekiel saw, just to employ men to help clean up just in Israel alone: *"Then those who live in the towns of Israel will go out and use the weapons for fuel and burn them up ... Men will be regularly employed to cleanse the land. Some will go through the land and, in addition to them; others will bury those who remain on the ground. At the end of the seven months they will begin their search. As they go through the land and one of them sees a human bone, he will set up a marker beside it until the gravediggers have buried it"* (Ezekiel 39:9, 14-15 NIV).

The gravediggers will have help in cleansing the land of dead bodies, for God will summon all the flesh-eating fowls of the earth to come and consume the flesh of these dead. *"And I saw an angel standing in the sun who cried in a loud voice to all the birds* *flying midair, come, gather together for the great supper of God, so that you may eat the flesh of kings, generals, and mighty men, of horses and their riders, **and the flesh of all people**, free and slave, small and great"* (Revelation 19:17-18 NIV).

It appears also that you will not see many large metropolises, for all of the skyscrapers and megacities will be destroyed in so much that *"...**every lofty tower and every fortified wall ...the arrogance of man shall be brought low** and the pride of men humbled; the Lord alone will be exalted in that day, and the idols will totally disappear"* (Isaiah 2:15-18 KJV). Also this additional Scripture in Isaiah seems to be speaking about the destruction of great cities with their high and lofty skyscrapers, *"In that day **their strong cities**, which they left because of the Israelites, **will be like places abandoned to thickets and undergrowth. And all will be desolate"*** (Isaiah 17:9 NIV). Because of the lack of major cities, factories, and mass industries, it can be assumed that the majority of the survivors will turn to farming, tilling the ground, and making a life with agriculture. You will also not see many industries, and most likely satellite communications will be nonexistent, as the great battle of Armageddon and the second coming of Christ would have put out all of the power grids, and industries that make weapons of steel, etc. will be gone. You will probably return to a seventeenth-century technology.

Russia's (Gog) future cemetery in Jerusalem

It's going to take most of the survivors a long of time to clean up this worldwide destruction in order to arrive at some level of habitability. One nation, in particular, that will experience a tremendous amount of dead soldiers will be Gog and Magog (Russia). The number of Russian soldiers that will be killed in the second coming will be so massive that God sections off a special burial ground or cemetery just for them—right in the land of Israel itself. In Ezekiel, God gives these Russians their very own burial grounds; *"On that day I will give Gog a burial place in Israel, in the valley of those who travel east toward the Sea. It will block the way of travelers, because Gog and all his hordes will be buried there. So it will be called the Valley of Hamon Gog"* (Ezekiel 39:11 NIV).

Russia will be severely punished for their leadership and manpower because of their plan to invade and destroy the Holy Land of Israel. Russia, along with Iran (Persia), will spearhead this invasion, but they will all be wiped out. Ironically, and I am jumping ahead a little when I say this, Russia will once again rise up, after the thousand-year reign of Jesus Christ, to attempt to overthrow the beloved City of Jerusalem. With their massive armies they will encompass the saints of the living God. This uprising will not last very long, for God will shower fire from heaven upon them and devour them all. This surely will be the end of all wicked plots and schemes devised by Gog and Magog forever. *"And when the thousand years are expired, Satan shall be loosed out of his prison, and he shall go out to deceive the nations which are in the four quarters of the earth, Gog and Magog, to gather them to battle: the number of whom is as the sands of the sea"* (Revelation 20:7-8 NIV). It is appropriate to note here that there is a vast number of Russian soldiers who advocate to the Muslim doctrine, which is anti-Semitic and against Christianity as well. So it is no wonder, that a nation made of atheistic leaders hungry for plunder, and armies that are hateful toward the Jews and Christian will merge.

The armies of Gog and Magog are scripturally represented with horses and horsemen rather than tanks, planes, jeeps, or other modern vehicles of war. The reasons for this can be many; however, the strongest of these reasons, as I previously said, lie within a nation's capability of taking out another country's power grids. Once a first-world nation takes out an opposing army's ability to generate electrical or electronic powers; they are completely without power. All tanks, planes, satellites, vehicles, missiles, city power systems are all reliant upon computers. And the USA, as well as many other powerful nations, have the capabilities of destroying power grids that can black out an entire geographical area and can possibly force a nation or the entire world into a seventeenth-century technology, i.e., horses and horsemen. I would assume that during the thousand-year reign, very little rebuilding of power grids, at least initially, or any mass construction of military armaments will occur while Jesus sits upon His throne on earth.

Other possibilities could be the lack of interpreting twenty-first-century technologies that could not be described by the biblical writers, so they could only refer to a vehicle as a horse, because there was no vocabulary for tank, car, truck, or jeep. Another possibility could be that there are tanks, cars, and other vehicles present, but writers like John or Ezekiel referred only to the horses in the battle because many of the mountainous areas of the Middle East are made up of impassable roads for vehicles. Many will be forced to use horses, as American soldiers have used in the past while warring against the Taliban in Afghanistan, for instance.

WHAT HAPPENS TO ALL THE FALLEN ANGELS?

Most of the fallen angels are either cast into the lake of fire for punishment or chained until their final release. They, for the most part, will be chained and cast into an abyss along with Satan until the thousand years is over. Their judgment is forever; these fallen angels will never receive mercy for what they have done by rebelling in heaven against God and tormenting the inhabitants of the earth for thousands of years. Just like the angels of heaven were used to punish the wicked humans on the earth during the second coming, these same angels are used to round up all of the fallen angels inhabiting the earth, *"And I looked and turned to another part of the earth, and saw there a deep valley with burning fire. And they brought the kings and the mighty, and began to cast them into this deep valley. And there mine eyes saw how they made these instruments, iron chains of immeasurable weight. And I asked the angel* of peace who *went with me, saying:* **For whom are these chains being prepared? And he said unto me: These are being prepared for the host of Azazel, so that they may take them and cast them into the abyss of complete condemnation, and they shall cover their jaws with rough stones as the Lord of Spirits commanded. And Michael, and Gabriel, and Raphael, and Phanuel shall take hold of them on that great day, and cast them on that day into the burning furnace, that the Lord of Spirits may take vengeance on them for their unrighteousness in becoming subject to Satan and leading astray those who dwell on the earth"** (Enoch 54:1-6).

There is also another a section I discovered that leads the reader to believe that casting these fallen angels into the abyss is not permanent, and that they are to remain there until the final great judgment as I alluded above. *"And again the Lord said to Raphael: Bind Azazel hand and foot, and cast him into darkness: and make an opening in the desert, which is in Dudael (the caldron of God), and cast him therein. And place him upon rough and jagged rocks, and cover him with darkness, and let him abide there forever, and cover his face that he may not see light. And on the day of the great judgment he shall be cast into the fire. And heal the earth, which the angels have corrupted, and proclaim healing of the earth, that they may heal the plague, and that all the children of men may not perish through all the secret things that the Watchers have disclosed and have taught their sons. The whole earth has been corrupted through the works of Azazel: to him ascribe all sin.* **Bind them fast for seventy generations in the valleys of the earth till the day of their judgment and** *of their consummation, till the judgment that is forever and forever is consummated"* (Enoch 10:4-8, 12).

All of these fallen angels are actually evil spirits or demons that are part of a hierarchy throughout the earth that have tempted and tormented mankind since the time of Adam and Eve. Enoch actually refers to a few fallen angels by name, and one in particular is the demonic serpent in the garden that tempted Eve to eat from the tree of knowledge and of good and evil. *"And the third was named Gadreel: he it is who showed the children of men all the blows of death, **and he led astray Eve,** and showed the weapons of death"* (Enoch 69:6). Another fallen angel that is mentioned by Enoch is Kasdeja: *"And the fifth was named Kasdeja: this is he who showed the children of men all the wicked smittings of spirits and demons, and the smittings of the embryo in the womb, that it may pass away, and the smittings of the soul the bites of the serpent, and the smittings which befall through the noontide heat, the son of the serpent named Tabaet"* (Enoch 69:12).

As we all have been taught, the lake of fire was never meant for mankind, for the eternal fire was actually reserved for only the devil and his fallen angels (Matthew 25:41). Though we will discuss this in our fourth chapter, it was never a predestination of God to send man to any place but heaven, which is eternal life. There is an eternal fire that will never be quenched and neither shall the sufferings of the damned ever cease—day or night (Mark 4:43-44). Regretfully many a man will find their final eternity in a fervent lake of fire, originally designed for demons, wicked spirits, Satan and his fallen angels.

THERE WILL BE MASSIVE GEOGRAPHICAL CHANGES IN OUR GLOBES AND MAPS

You will be shocked to see, as a survivor, that the aftermath of the second coming will extremely alter the geographical landscape of the globe as we know it today, both positively and negatively. And these geographical changes will tremendously affect those who survive His return. Maps will need to be rethought; mountains and islands that we see now may not be there in the future. Roads, highways, bridges, and probably entire cities may be obliterated. Landmarks, historical structures, bodies of water, and even seasonal climate and weather, the equator, polar caps, and hemispheres may not exist, or at least not as you remember them.

Earth's geography will certainly experience incredibly positive changes. For instance, once Jesus actually touches His feet onto the Mount of Olives, the mountaintop will split in two, much like what can happen in an earthquake. This split will form a great valley (Zechariah 14:3-4), which will form two new rivers that will flow from out of the city of Jerusalem's walls. But these are not just any common rivers. They are referred to as "living waters," for they are life-giving waters to all of the people who can drink from them. The waters will be medicinal, youth invigorating, and holy. These waters will be giving life to the people as well as to the ecology. (See Zechariah 14:8.)

Other geographical changes to the earth will concern topography of Israel. First, God will cause a massive enlargement of the Temple Mount. It will be heightened to become the chief mountain (Micah 4:1) of all Israel. The city of Jerusalem will also be greatly widened and shall become the most important city in the world (as well as the central capital.) When one deciphers the measurements of the newly enlarged Jerusalem, its width can span from Los Angeles to Denver, CO. This is where Jesus will be headquartered and His throne will sit in the new temple, which will dwarf all prior temples and the Tabernacle in the wilderness put together. You will read this in more detail in Chapter 3.

The throne in which He will sit will be situated in the Holiest of Holies of the temple, and there he will place His feet and live there among the Jewish people. *"While the man was standing beside me, I heard someone speaking to me from inside the temple. He said: 'Son of man, **this is the place of my throne and the place for the soles of my feet. This is where I will live among the Israelites forever.** The house of Israel will never again defile my holy name – neither they nor their kings – by their prostitution and the lifeless idols of their kings at their high places"* (Ezekiel 43:6-7 NIV). There, in the temple, the entire government of the world will rest upon the shoulders of Jesus Christ: *"...**And the government will be on His shoulders.** And He will be called Wonderful Counselor, Mighty God, Everlasting Father, and Prince of Peace. Of the increase of His government and peace there will be no end. He will reign on David's throne and over his kingdom, establishing and upholding it with justice and righteousness from that time on and forever. The zeal of the Lord Almighty will accomplish this"* (Isaiah 9:6-7 NIV).

The geography of Jerusalem will be likened literally unto the *Garden of Eden,* a most beautiful and positive geographical change to be sure. *"The Lord will surely comfort Zion and will look with compassion on all her ruins; he will make her **deserts like Eden, her wastelands like the garden of the Lord**. Joy and gladness will be found in her; thanksgiving, and the sound of singing"* (Isaiah 51:3 NIV).

THERE WILL BE MAJOR CHANGES IN DAYLIGHT AND NIGHTTIME

You will witness also another most amazing climatic change over the temple mount itself: *"Then the Lord will create over all Mount Zion and over those who assemble there **a cloud of smoke by day and a glow of flaming fire by night; over all the glory will be a canopy. It will be a shelter and shade from the heat of day, and a refuge and hiding place from the storm and rain"*** (Isaiah 4:5-6 NIV). You might recall reading in the book of Exodus that while the Hebrews wandered the wilderness for forty years in the desert, they followed a cloud by day and a pillar of fire by night. The fire and the cloud not only gave them direction but also provided a shade by day from the hot desert sun, and a warm light by night to help them see where they were walking. This will also happen over the temple. All of the temple workers and people that visit will see this divine cloud by day and a ring of fire by night.

Some extravagant changes in the weather will be the incredible increase in the brightness of the sun and moon, *"The moon will shine like the sun, and the sunlight will be* **seven times brighter, like the light of seven full days,** *when the Lord binds up the bruises of His people and heals the wounds He inflicted"* (Isaiah 30:26 NIV). Notice that the sun is seven times brighter and not hotter. Evidently the power of the sun to bring accelerated health and growth to the ecology and to the people will be seven times more potent. In other words, what the sun can do for a field of crops in seven days presently, the sun will accomplish the same in just one day during the millennium. Because of the enormous downpour of nutrients the sun provides, the agriculture and the ecosystems will prove to be amazing indeed.

WHY IS GOD SO ANGRY OR AVENGING?

One might ask why God is so angry and why is His wrath not coupled with mercy? These are fair questions, but when we consider that we have seen two entire world civilizations: the civilization before the Great Flood that left only eight human survivors on the earth, and the worldwide civilization after the flood (ending at the second coming) where not many shall survive. Both civilizations have committed great abominations before the Lord. As we have seen, the second civilization shall be destroyed by the wrath of God during Jesus' return, leaving a third civilization that will live during the next 1000 years; this civilization also shall end with the rebellion of mankind, and there shall be no survivors. A fourth and final civilization will be gleaned from all of these prior civilizations to live an immortal life with God and Christ for all of eternity in heaven.

Here are two reasons why God is, at the point of Jesus' return, so very angry:

First, in Genesis 6:3, God emphatically states that His Spirit will "not contend" (or put up with) with mortal man and his indiscriminate wickedness and evil forever. For God, there was an end in sight for all mankind since the first book of the Bible was ever written. Once man has been taken into His presence in Heaven for all eternity, we as immortal beings are no longer homo sapiens. Again, there is an end in the mind of God for mortal humans. We will be spirit-beings, just like God is. The finality of mankind as terrestrial earthlings should not come as a surprise to any of us, for there will be an end of the world, as we know it. Amos says that God is "pressed under" *by the sins of the world* (Amos 2:13 KJV). Isaiah says that God is "wearied" by the sins of the world (Isaiah 43:24). Ezekiel says that God is broken by the sins of mankind (Ezekiel 6:9). And the writer of Genesis states that God can be grieved by the sins of the world (Genesis 6:6).

God's nature has been longsuffering, merciful, full of grace and love toward us, so much so that it cannot be measured in human terms. However, God's anger is likened to a cup that is filling slowly to the brim, and once the cup is full, there must be a reckoning. *"They too, will drink of the wine of God's fury, which has been poured full strength into the cup of His wrath..."* (Revelation 14:10 NIV). Revelation 16:19 also mention the cup of God's wrath. There is just so much of man's sin which God's cup can hold before it runs over. As a smaller example, in Genesis 15:16

(KJV), Moses states, *"The iniquity of the Amorites are not yet full."* And although the Amorites pushed the envelope and incurred God's wrath, the Scripture reflects God's mercy and slowness to angry.

Secondly, God has promised that He will avenge those who were martyred for God's sake. God's inordinate mercy is so longsuffering that it frustrates those martyrs that stand around the throne of God crying for their avenging. *"When he opened the fifth seal, I saw under the altar the souls of those who had been slain because of the word of God and the testimony they had maintained. They called out in a loud voice, **how long, Sovereign Lord, holy and true, until you judge the inhabitants of the earth and avenge our blood?"** *(Revelation 6:9-10 NIV). They were told to wait until a further number of their fellow servants and brothers who were to be killed were added to them in heaven.

The holiness of God will ultimately be reconciled through the judgment of all of our sins, or be shielded by the blood of Jesus Christ and His propitiation. Make no mistake, every man's sins must be reconciled, either through his own personal eternal punishment or through salvation in Jesus Christ, the Savior of the world. Everyone has been given the power of a free will; to make a personal choice to follow Jesus Christ or choose not to. Evil has been placed into this world in order to draw a clear line between what is good and what is bad. God Gave commandments and laws in order to show what God says are sins and not sins. Without the Law we would not know what displeases Him. Satan actually has been placed between God and us as a tool of God in order for us to choose the ways of the wicked or to choose the way of Christ as a believer. Neurosurgeon Eben Alexander, who authored the book *Proof of Heaven,* said this: *"Evil was necessary because without it free will was impossible, and without free will there could be no growth – no forward movement, no chance for us to become what God longed for us to be.*

Horrible and all-powerful as evil sometimes seems to be in a world like ours, in the larger picture love was overwhelmingly dominant, and it would ultimately be triumphant."

His Iron Scepter and
the Surviving Population

If you are a survivor, you will certainly see that once Jesus has arrived physically upon the earth, and all wickedness has been destroyed, Jesus will set up His Kingdom, ruling the remaining population of the world with an iron scepter (Revelation 19:15).

The iron scepter rule of law is indicative of how Jesus will reign during His new world order. His rule will be aggressive, absolute, forceful, uncompromising, and intolerant. As I mentioned prior, though there are no unbelievers on the earth, there will eventually be non-receivers of His rule of order. And for these rebellious people (and I pray that you are not numbered among them), there will be immediate consequences metered out against them with extreme measures. This rule will not be a democracy, or a republic; His rule will be a theocracy. He will have zero tolerance for the rebellious persons or nations. As we shall see in chapter 3, Jesus will present the Kingdom of God to the Almighty Father once He has placed all his enemies under His feet. *"Then the end will come, when He hands over the Kingdom to God the Father after He has destroyed all dominion, authority and power"* (1 Corinthians 15:24 NIV).

The arrival of God's wrath will appease the prophets as well as the general population. For instance, Habakkuk had a serious complaint with God's longsuffering and mercy, and it caused frustration with this prophet because the wicked were literally getting away with murder and violence. *"How long O Lord, must I call for help, but you don't listen? Or cry out to you, Violence! But you do not save? Why do you make me look at injustice? Why do you tolerate wrong? Destruction and violence are before me;*

there is strife, and conflict abounds. Therefore the law is paralyzed, and justice never prevails. The wicked hem in the righteous, so that justice is perverted" (Habakkuk 1:2-4 NIV). I think we all can relate to Habakkuk's frustration as he watches wicked and evil people do whatever they want without consequence or any divine intervention. Habakkuk continues his complaint and says, *"Your eyes are too pure to look on evil; you cannot tolerate wrong. Why then do you tolerate the treacherous? Why are you silent while the wicked swallow up those more righteous than themselves?"* (Habakkuk 1:13 NIV). The prophet goes back and forth with God in all of his frustrations with the evils of this world and with God's seemingly endless mercies. It's not that we should rejoice at the destruction of others, but we can feel vindicated and protected by God when He judges a person or nation for their crimes against society. When justice reigns and the wicked are punished, then the world has order.

Jesus' new world order will have a righteous and holy leadership where all creation can flourish. I will mention this again in a later chapter, but haven't we heard all too often, "Why does God tolerate all of this evil?" Or "Why does God let bad things happen to good people?" Well the arrival of this avenging King will put a stop to all of evil, and no harm will befall any good people. But are we prepared to see the level to which God must act to see these questions appeased?

Personally, I have wept for the wicked, the unbeliever and the lost of my community here in Houston. I am not one that shouts with base satisfaction, "You'll get yours! You are going to get what you deserve!" On the contrary. I do not want to see anyone perish upon His return. Those who share end times Scriptures with a vengeful attitude is missing the whole point of the gospel: that it is not God's will that any should perish, and neither should it be our will. May God continue His longsuffering and mercy.

Chapter Two

Jesus' Thousand-Year New World Order

"I beheld till the thrones were cast down, and the Ancient of days did sit, whose garment was white as snow, and His hair of His head like pure wool: His throne was like the fiery flame, and His wheels as burning fire."

(Daniel 7:9 KJV)

There will be no more presidents, prime ministers, highnesses, kings, queens, princes or princesses, dictators, tribal rulers, popes, ambassadors, rogue leaders, or dignitaries that will remain standing in the aftermath of Jesus' return. His invasion marks the moment in which all national and world leadership is totally taken over by Christ.

As a survivor, you will immediately notice that the reign of Jesus Christ will create a unique society of leadership in that many of His leaders will be those who were previously raptured (resurrected) and thus immortal. *"Then the sovereignty and power and greatness of the kingdoms under the whole heaven will be handed over to the saints, the people of the Most High. His kingdom will be an everlasting kingdom, and all the rulers will worship and obey Him"* (Daniel 7:27 NIV). Daniel is clear here that these saints are those who arose from their sleep or death. *"As for you, go your way till the end. You will rest, and then at the end of days you will rise to receive your allotted inheritance"* (Daniel 12:13 NIV). The inheritance, which Jesus spoke of, can consist of being a king or priest, or, more specific to what Jesus told us, to inherit five or ten cities on the earth (Luke 19:17).

The beginning of the thousand-year reign of Jesus Christ will actually mark the third human civilization (pre-flood, post-flood, and post-second coming) and the last. The great flood that washed away all of civilization was used by Jesus Himself as a comparison to the great and terrible return of the Christ: *"As it was in the days of Noah, so it will be at the coming of the Son of Man. For in the days before the flood, people were eating and drinking, marrying and giving in marriage, up to the day when Noah entered the ark; and they knew nothing about what would happen until the flood came and took them all away. That is how it will be at the coming of the Son of Man"* (Matthew 24:37-39 NIV). Only eight souls were spared in the worldwide destruction by the great flood, and I sadly suspect that a minority of the human race will survive the return of Jesus Christ (Matthew 7:13), much like occurred during the great flood. This last civilization of humankind will mark the last chance for humankind to make the right decision to love the Lord with all of their heart, soul, mind, and strength. This last civilization will be led much differently than the previous two, for the Son of God and His Bride, the Church, will rule them.

Joel, the Old Testament prophet, explains that both before and *during* the millennium there will be big decisions that need to be made by the numerous multitudes of men throughout the whole world: will they choose to believe in the God of Abraham, Isaac, and Jacob, and the Son of God, or will they reject Him? *"Multitudes, multitudes in the valley of decision! For the day of the LORD is near in the valley of decision"* (Joel 3:14 KJV). If you are a survivor of the second coming, then this Scripture directly applies to you. Notice that the decision is related to the great and terrible day of the Lord and not a poorly selected Scripture taken out of context. It is crystal clear here that it is a matter of making an emphatic and resolved decision for Christ, and not a predetermined destiny for those who are going to be selected for heaven and for those who are selected to be sent to the lake of eternal fire. No, this is the gift God has given us, the gift of free choice–deciding personally to elect Christ.

Amazingly, as a survivor, all of your holy leaders (priests) and political leaders (kings) will be honest and selfless. They will be immortal, raptured folks who truly represent the King of the earth, and they will serve Him at His pleasure. This will be a refreshing change for the inhabitants of the earth. Imagine being able to trust a national leader or a preacher. There is an old saying that when you are in company, avoid conversing about religion and politics. However, during the thousand years, speaking openly about the government and religion will be the rule rather than the avoided exception. Being politically correct will be nonsense, for the truth will be propagated throughout the world without fear of punishment. There will not be any opposing political parties, riots, or rallies revolting against His government. Everyone will love and have faith in the decisions made by Jesus Christ and His selected leaders.

THE AWARDED AUTHORITY TO GOVERN WITH THE KING

The raptured saints will reign with Jesus over the small, surviving human society, and this will include you (as part of the surviving society, not as a raptured saint.) When Daniel wrote of the great and terrible day of the Lord's second coming, he said that he was deeply troubled and that *his face turned pale* for those who will not survive (Daniel 7:28). Nevertheless, Daniel wrote joyfully concerning the saints that would reign in the kingdom of God after the destruction of the wicked and the unbelievers. As a survivor, you will notice that the saints will be privileged to receive many rewards based upon their good deeds they performed while on the earth. As I mentioned in the introduction, there will be crowns, thrones, and white robes for those who have accomplished much. In a book found among the Old Testament Pseudepigrapha Volume 2, called the Martyrdom and Ascension of Isaiah 9:24-26, it reads: *"And I saw many robes placed there, and many thrones and many crowns, and I said to the angel who led me, 'Whose are these robes and thrones and crowns'? And he said to me, 'As for these robes, there are many from the world who will receive them through believing in the words of that one who will be named as I have told you, and they will keep them, and believe in them, and believe in His cross; for them these are placed here."*

But there will be very little to nothing for those who were saved but lacked in accomplishments or services for the kingdom. God has set up a reward-based system for those who emerge victorious and are taken in the rapture. Jesus Christ Himself provides the rewards as He takes control of the earth: *"And behold I come quickly;* and my reward is with Me, to give every man according to his work shall be"* (Revelation 22:12-13 KJV). Jesus will be returning to the earth, not just with the wrath of God against the wicked, but with all of the rewards and promotions for those who have done great things at great personal sacrifice for the sake of those who were needy and for the tenets of Christianity. The rewards and promotions are given to the raptured saints only, and they will be those from the time of Adam and Eve through the days of tribulation, when many will be killed or martyred for the name of Christ. These rewards are related to crowns, which signify divine-given authority upon the earth during His reign.

There is a wonderful insight provided in one of Jesus' parables concerning the rewards and authority bestowed upon those who return from the rapture: *"Well done, my good servant! His* *master replied. Because you have been trustworthy in a very small matter, **take charge of ten cities.** The second came and said, sir your mina has earned five more. His master answered, **you take charge of five cities***" (Luke 19:1-19 NIV). It appears here that some of the raptured saints will inherit a number of cities under their authority during the millennium. This is pertinent considering these cities are populated by mortals and will be governed by immortals. This is a vast improvement, as I mentioned, from the present politicians and many of those who claim to be in the ministry, but are actually serving for their own profit. These immortal governors will certainly represent righteousness and will work directly for King Jesus as ambassadors who are headquartered in Jerusalem.

A clearer peek at how God will judge and reward a man's works is given to us by Paul in his letter to the Corinthian church, "*If any man builds on this foundation using gold, silver, costly stones, wood, hay, or straw, his work shall be shown for what it is, because the **Day** will bring it to light. It will be revealed with fire, and the fire will test the quality of each man's work. If what he has built survives, he will receive his reward. If it is burned up, he will suffer loss; **he himself will be saved, but only as one escaping through the flames***" (1 Corinthians 3:12-15 KJV).

Obviously some who will be raptured will not fare very well in the final analysis because of their lack of quality works. The beatitudes mentions, for instance, that the meek will inherit the earth (Matthew 5:5), and this inheritance is speaking of the millennial period in which authority is given to those who are meek and not easily provoked to anger, but are the patient, the courteous, the generous, the tempered spirited, and those less likely to be mean-spirited, envious, or proud. I believe a meek spirit will survive the test of fire among many other God-like characteristics we practiced while upon the earth. The godly characteristics and traits that we assume are actually what make us good. Indeed, these qualities make us a better person.

However, if you are a human survivor, you are not a candidate for any of these rewards or any authority for that matter, for your blessing is manifested in your very survival. You were spared. Though you will be considered blessed because you have survived, your actual role on the earth will be to obey the rule of law of the King, and to remain steadfastly obedient even in the face of those who will eventually rebel against His world government. During your tenure upon the earth, you will be eventually tested and judged to determine whether you will enter the gates of Heaven at the close of the thousand years. This is to be your central goal.

What exactly are Jesus' constitutional laws for His new world order?

I am sure you have heard it said, "How can a good God allow such bad things to happen to good people? Where is the justice?" Actually the prophets of the Old Testament asked this and other questions as well. The answers to these questions are actually answered and acted upon during the reign and new world order of King Jesus. There will be zero-tolerance for those who would hurt others or act in wickedness.

Jesus' constitutional law that will govern all the surviving humans (and for all nations) will be the reinstating of the Ten Commandments and Torah (the first five books of the Old Testament). The Ten Commandments are quite common to most and have been the foundation of our laws for several generations here in the USA as well as other civilizations throughout the world. These laws include: worshipping only one God who is the God of Abraham, Isaac, and Jacob, not possessing any idols, not using God's name in vain, observing the Sabbath, honoring your parents, not to murder, not to commit adultery, not to steal, lie, or covet. Enoch mentions that the law will be in place for the duration of the millennium and up to the time of the new earth. *"And the angel Uriel showed me their laws exactly as they are, and how it is with regard to all the years of the world and unto eternity, till the new creation is accomplished which endured till eternity"* (Enoch 72:1).

Every mortal inhabitant will know the truth about God Almighty, His Son Jesus Christ, and His Holy Spirit, *"For the earth will be filled with the knowledge of the glory of the Lord, as the waters cover the sea"* (Habakkuk 2:14). Ironically, there will be those who will eventually be non-receivers of God's glory or, more explicitly, they will not obey Jesus' new world order and laws. *"Though grace is shown to the wicked, they do not learn righteousness; even in a land of uprightness they go on doing evil and regard not the majesty of the Lord"* (Isaiah 26:10 NIV). They will not embrace Jesus' rule, and some will even grow to hate Him, turning against His kingdom and laws, as the population of the earth quickly grows and each generation follows.

One specific law that Jesus will require of all nations is a mandatory annual pilgrimage to Jerusalem in order to celebrate and worship Him during the Feasts of Tabernacles. Some of the nations that will rebel against the King will consequently refuse to honor this pilgrimage. Zechariah warns that those who refuse to come to Jerusalem will be punished with a drought and famine. *"The survivors from all the nations will go up year after year to worship the King, the Lord Almighty, and to celebrate the Feast of Tabernacles. If any of the peoples of the earth do not go up to Jerusalem to worship the King, the Lord Almighty, **they will have no rain**"* (Zechariah 14:16-17 NIV).

It is beyond my imagination that any person or nation would not feel the need to honor and worship Jesus Christ in person during this annual pilgrimage. When you consider that Satan is no longer an influence on the earth (because he has been cast into the bottomless pit), and the Antichrist and false prophet having been cast into the lake of fire, then what remains are only man's fleshly desires, rebellion, and pride. Although they were not qualified to be raptured, I believe that these wayward, surviving mortals initially will not be rebellious after the second coming. During their continuing life into the thousand years, evidently, they will fall into a wicked state, unprovoked by evil spirits, but influenced by their own rebellious nature.

Let me advise you that if you survive and are found in a nation that is rebelling against the King, move out of that nation and into one that honors and obeys the Lord. Too often in our history, God has punished nations because of the foolish and ungodly decisions their respective leaders make for them, and during the millennial period, this will be no different. Entire nations that do not observe Jesus' policies, or God's laws, will be punished—citizens and leaders alike—as all too often, the propaganda of leadership persuades citizens to agree with them. You might ask, if there are immortal leaders of nations, how do these nations rebel? Once again, everyone will have the ability to make their own personal decision to live for God or refuse. Even though there will be immortal leadership, this will not stop those who will rebel and then find and gather adherents to their rebellion. Regretfully, punishment will come quickly to those nations that will turn against God.

JESUS AND THE JEWS WILL
TEACH THE LAW TO YOU

During the new world order, Jesus will reinstitute and teach the Law, which you and the whole world will be expected to adhere to. However, all the nations of the world will be joyful to assemble themselves to hear Him teach Torah and how it relates to His covenant, about the Almighty God, the fulfillment of His promises, the Old Testament types and shadows, the fulfillment of prophesies, and what is good and evil in the eyes of God. The minor prophet Micah expresses how the nations will be drawn to the temple mount to be personally instructed by Jesus Christ during the thousand years: *"Many Nations shall come and say, come let us go to the mountain of the Lord, to house of the God of Jacob. He will teach us His ways, so that we may walk in His paths. The Law will go out in Zion, the word of the Lord from Jerusalem"* (Micah 4:2 NIV).

Jews and Gentiles are still very much tied with biblical covenants and laws and teachings. Notice what Jesus says here when He refers to a man that keeps the law during the millennium: *"Do not think that I have come to abolish the Law or the Prophets; I have come to fulfill them. I tell you the truth, until heaven and earth disappear, not the smallest letter, not the least stroke of a pen, will by any means disappear from the Law until everything is accomplished. **Anyone who breaks one of the least of these commandments and teaches others to do the same will be called least in the kingdom of heaven. But whoever practices and teaches these commandments will be called great in the kingdom of heaven"** (Matthew 5:17-19 NIV).

The kingdom of heaven that Jesus is referring to is the millennial reign kingdom of Jesus Christ, and the Law He is referring to is the first five books of the Old Testament (Torah), which, more specifically, includes the Ten Commandments. You also may have noticed, according to Jesus, that the Law will not disappear until all of heaven and earth has disappeared. To be put simply, the Law is with us until God destroys this earth and replaces it with a brand new one, and this will not happen until after the thousand years are complete.

Amazingly, Jewish people during the thousand years will be sought after by the unlearned Gentiles in order to be taught the Law of God. This, of course, is a drastic shift from history in that Jews throughout the ages have typically been sought for extermination, persecution, or relocation. *"This is what the Almighty says: in those days ten men from all languages and nations will take firm hold of one Jew by the hem of his robe and say, let us go with you, because we have heard that God is with you"* (Zechariah 8:23 NIV). You should, as a survivor, take this Scripture personally and seek out the Jewish population, not just to learn about the Word of God and His covenant promises, but also to gain a closer proximity to Jesus through revelation and education. I don't know if it will be possible for you, but if you are a survivor, you might want to consider relocating to Israel in order to have many of these amenities available to you. In Israel, Jewish teachers will be more abundant, the temple is located there, all of Israel will be compared to the Garden of Eden, and since all nations are required to make the annual pilgrimage to Jerusalem during the Feasts of Tabernacles, your travels will be minimal. Moreover, the greatest blessing of living in Israel would be the physical closeness of King Jesus.

The new world order will see God return to His chosen people, the Jews. The second return of Jesus Christ will mark the end of the ***time of the Gentiles*** (Luke 21:24; Romans 11:25) and Jesus will be physically living among the Jews in Jerusalem as their King. But do not think for one moment that Jesus will turn His back upon the Gentiles, for He will merge His elect children with the Jews, and all of us will be known as His people, *"Shout and be glad, O daughter of Zion. **For I am coming, and will live among you,** declares the Lord. **Many nations will be joined** with the Lord in that day and will become my people. **I will live among you** and you will know that the Lord Almighty has sent Me to you"* (Zechariah 2:10-11 NIV). As you may know, the Jews initially rejected Jesus as the Son of God, so God turned His attention to the non-Jews or Gentiles, and this became known as the time of the Gentiles.

Salvation was first offered to the Jews as a clear advantage to them, *"For I am not ashamed of the gospel, because it is the power of God* *that brings salvation of everyone who believes: **first to the Jew, then for the Gentile***" (Romans 1:16 NIV). Jesus while prophesying of the end of times stated that there would be a time when the Jews would initially reject the gospel. As a matter of fact, many of the Hebrews were and are, blinded of the salvation of Jesus Christ by God Almighty Himself, *"**For the others were hardened,** just as it is written, **God gave them a spirit of stupor,** eyes to see not and ears to hear not, down to this very day"* (Romans 11:7-8 NIV). You can also find this setting of scripture alluded to in Deuteronomy 29:4 and Isaiah 29:9-10. Though a minority of the Hebrews accepted and will accept the gospel, the vast remainder did not choose Christ because God gave them over to their own inclinations. God will not contend with a man forever, be he Jew or Gentile, if He consistently rejects Him, for He will turn them over to their own desires, allow them to be steered to a reprobate mind, to not know God or even try to retain Him in their minds. (See Romans 1:21, 24-26, 28.) The gospel consequently was openly and expressly offered to the Gentiles for a season, and that Jerusalem would be trampled upon until the *"time of the gentiles are fulfilled"* (Luke 21:24). The time of the Gentiles will be fulfilled once the thousand-year reign of Jesus Christ begins, and then God will once again turn to His people, the Jews. As a survivor, this will directly affect you in so much as the Jews will be used in the temple at the return of the Levitical services and the holy Jewish priests, and the Jewish community being known to be the people of God and teachers of the Torah. Seek these people out to become knowledgeable of the Word of God and the Laws of God.

WILL THERE BE THE RETURNING TWELVE TRIBES OF ISRAEL?

You will discover, as a survivor, especially if you are living in Israel, that Jesus will reunify the tribes of Israel, and establish tribal land boundaries much like they had after the occupation of the Promised Land under the leadership of Joshua (Isaiah 11:11). Originally, the Jews took occupation of Israel after forty years of wandering in the wilderness. The Jewish leadership divided up the entire land of Israel into sections, giving each of the twelve tribes of Israel its respective land mass, except for the tribe of Levi. The Levites were given the role of temple keepers and their inheritance was to live in and around the temple area, supported by the other eleven tribes.

Is David made prince over the Jews for the thousand years?

Some students of the Bible believe that King David will be resurrected at the rapture and placed as prince over the heritage of the Jews in Jerusalem after the return of Christ. Other theorists believe that the name David is referring to Jesus Christ, who is occupying the throne of David in Jerusalem during the thousand years. *"I will place over them one shepherd, my servant David, and he will tend them; he will tend to them and be their shepherd. I the Lord will be their God, and my servant David will be prince among them. I the Lord have spoken"* (Ezekiel 34:23-24 NIV). Because there seems to be a difference between the "Lord" and the "prince," it is plausible that the Lord Jesus Christ shall rule as Lord over the world, and David will be the prince over the city of Jerusalem or the nation of Israel. As we know clearly, King David will be among those who will be raptured and shall rule with Christ for a thousand years, so this hypothesis is not a real stretch for me.

Ezekiel also mentions the leadership appointment of His servant David in chapter 37: *"My servant David will be king over them, and they will all have one shepherd. They will follow my laws and be careful to keep my decrees. They will live in the land I gave to my servant Jacob, the land where your fathers lived. They and their children will live there forever, and David my servant will be their prince forever"* (Ezekiel

37:24-25 NIV). When Ezekiel wrote these Scriptures, King David was already dead and buried many years prior, so this is not a prophesy of the first David who slew Goliath and ruled over Israel. This is the David who will come back after the rapture.

Whether this prophesy speaks of King David of old, or refers to Jesus using the name David interchangeably, I don't know conclusively. But personally, I lean toward the prince being King David because of the lack of upper case letters used by Ezekiel. If you compare Isaiah 9:6 you will note that *"Prince of Peace"* describing Jesus Christ is in upper case lettering. Also, I believe that Jesus is the King of all Kings on the earth during this millennial, making David the prince of only the Jews. When you visit Jerusalem each year, you will possibly see the biblical King David as the prince of Israel alongside Jesus Christ who will reign as the King of Kings over the entire earth.

THE NEW WORLD ORDER WILL
SEE NEW LAWS OF NATURE

During Jesus' new world order, there will not be any harm done to anyone unless the King of Kings imputes it. No human will physically hurt another, and if one does hurt a person, he or she will have to contend with Jesus Christ, who with His iron scepter, will punish those who oppress (Jeremiah 30:19-20). For that matter, mankind will not see any more wars or weapons of warfare (Isaiah 2:4). There will not be any carnivorous or predatory animals like the lion, tiger, or panther (Isaiah 11:6-8, 65:25) for they will be given to eat the fruit of the earth and not blood. There will be no vipers or snakes that will bite anyone, including children playing near them, or even scorpions (Isaiah 11:6-8). Even death will become uncommon for the surviving humans and for their offspring. If a man dies at the age of one hundred years old, he will be considered but a child. And actually, the death of a child will be nonexistent. *"Never again will there be in it an infant who lives but a few days, or an old man who does not live out his years; the one who dies at a hundred will be thought a mere child; the one who fails to reach a hundred will be considered accursed"* (Isaiah 65:20, NIV).

Something more about animals upon the earth: the writer Baruch mentions that the wild animals that live in the forests, jungles, and woods will actually volunteer themselves in order to assist the survivors in their daily burdens and services. *"And the wild beasts will come from the wood and serve men, and the asps and dragons will come out of their holes to subject themselves to a child"* (2 Baruch 73:6). There will be no need for "breaking" or training a horse or a donkey, or even an ox–for they will all know how to serve mankind and do it willingly. I am persuaded to believe that other animals that man has not used to assist in farming and labor will be used as well.

I wanted to add here also that Baruch uses words that are quite comforting and even poetic in his description of the health, human attitudes, and conditions among the survivors: *"And it will happen after he has brought down everything which is in the world, and has sat down in eternal peace on the throne of the kingdom, then joy will be revealed and rest will appear.* ***And then health will descend in dew, and illness will vanish***, *and fear and tribulation and lamentation will pass away from among men, and joy will encompass the earth. And nobody again will die untimely, nor will any adversity take place suddenly. Judgment, condemnations, contentions, revenges, blood, passions, zeal, hate, and all such things will go into condemnation since they will be uprooted..."* (2 Baruch 73:1-5).

I really appreciate the way Baruch describes human health actually coming down *in dew*, not *like dew*. Somehow, health will pour down in the dew itself and sickness completely vanishes away. Actually, all sicknesses, diseases, and blindness will be virtually removed from mankind as well (Micah 4:6-7; Isaiah 35:5-6). For the lame will walk, the deaf will hear, the blind will see, and the dumb will speak. You will witness and probably be a participant of a tremendous surge of childbirths throughout the world, for to have many children will once again be considered a blessings of the Lord. I also appreciate the way Jeremiah the prophet describes how God will brighten the survivors' morale and return honor back into their lives. *"For them will come songs of thanksgiving and the sound of rejoicing. I will add to their numbers, and they will not be deceased; I will bring them honor, and they will not be distained. Their children will be as in days of old, and their community will be established before me; I will punish all that oppress them"* (Jeremiah 30:19-20 NIV).

Personally I have six biological children, whom I love so very much. Four of the six have their own homes, and two of my youngest still live with my wife and I. People have asked me throughout the years why I had so many children. Having many children means further financial burdens, less personal freedoms, and a loss of self-identity, because children take up much of your time and money. I, for one, have always looked at my many children (and presently four grandchildren) as shear blessings. I believe God will reestablish this perception during His new world order. Having many children will be considered a joy in a parent's life and not a hardship.

Survivors will find that even the curse directed to Eve in the Garden, in which childbirth would be painful, will be removed during Jesus' reign. *"And women will no longer have pain when they bear, nor will they be tormented when they yield the fruits of their womb"* (2 Baruch 73:2-3). I am confident that the lack of painful labor will be a further incentive for the families of the earth to rear more children than they would if risks of the health of the baby or mother were an issue. Those concerns will be put behind mankind once and for all. Too often today, abortions are considered for reasons of safety, health, financial issues, shame and guilt, or no desire for a child. Fortunately, these issues will not even enter into the minds of prospective moms and dads during the millennial reign of Christ.

FARMING AND LABORING WILL BE ANOTHER GARDEN OF EDEN

The soil (earth) that had been cursed for men's sake will be lifted, and thorns, thistles, and stony earth will not contend with the planter or sower any more. Indeed, the land (especially in Israel) will be referred to, in those days, as *the Garden of Eden* (Isaiah 51:3). All of nature will be restored and life for the inhabitants of the earth will be incredibly blessed, most likely under similar conditions that Adam and Eve experienced prior to their fall and expulsion.

As a survivor, you will be happy to know that men will love to go to work each day, and more than likely, the vast majority, if not all of mankind, will return once again to tilling the ground with a great sense of fulfillment. *"...My chosen ones will long enjoy the work of their hands* (Isaiah 65:22 NIV). Baruch also comments, and takes the joy of farming and laboring much further regarding the conditions of tilling the earth. *"And it will happen in those days that the reapers will not become tired, and the farmers will not wear themselves out, because the products of themselves will shoot out speedily, during the time that they work on them in full tranquility"* (2 Baruch 74:1). Evidently, fruits and vegetables will be growing very quickly for the reapers, maybe several days to just weeks after the seeds have been planted. And the seasons of certain fruit and vegetables may not be an issue any longer as well, for the sun and weather will be specifically conducive to farming. I so appreciate Baruch stating that the farmers will not grow weary and that there will be a speedy result of their light labors.

Consequently, you can expect to experience plenty of food, rain, and good soil to farm with. In the early nineteen hundreds, 80 percent of the country was agricultural and twenty percent worked in factories. However, once the Industrial Revolution took hold of our nation, there was a huge paradigm shift. Eighty percent of the work force went to work for mass production industries, and only twenty percent of the workforce made careers in farming. During the millennial reign, nearly all of the world will be working the fields– planting and harvesting.

Most of society will eat from what they plant, and drink from what they draw from the rivers. They will live in the houses they build with their own hands or occupy from what was left after the great day of the Lord. There will be no collection agencies, or high interest rates, or heavy mortgages, or financial institutions that can bankrupt you or repossess your house. For if a man builds a house for himself and his family, he will not have to fear losing it to a bank or a lender (Isaiah 65:21-22).

As you will discover, there will be no wars, no armies, no training for battles, nor will there be a marine, an airman, a soldier, or mercenary (and I suspect not even a police force or a security agency) to be found. All of the iron and other metals of the destroyed armor and weaponry will be used for farming equipment. *"He will judge between the nations and will settle disputes for many peoples. They will beat their swords into* **plowshares** *and their spears into* **pruning hooks**. *Nation will not take up sword against nation, nor will they train for war anymore"* (Isaiah 2:4 NIV). The prophet Enoch mentions that the actual use of metals will not even have much use during the thousand years on the earth outside of farming: *"And there shall be no iron for war, nor shall one clothe oneself with a breastplate. Bronze shall be of no service, and tin shall be of no service and shall not be esteemed, and lead shall not be desired. And all these things shall be denied and destroyed from the surface of the earth, when the Elect One shall appear before the face of the Lord of Spirits"* (Enoch 52:8-9). No doubt Enoch was speaking of the Elect One who is Jesus Christ, and He will not tolerate any mischief of battles or preparation of wars, or even the rumors of them.

A NEW FLOURISHING ECONOMY
FROM MIRACULOUS RIVERS

As I mentioned in chapter one, there will be major geographical changes to the earth's topography, especially in Israel (Zechariah 14:3-8; Isaiah 51:3). I also cited that there would be major changes in daytime and nighttime (Isaiah 4:5-6, 30:26). However, I reserved some further earth and climate change information for you in this section in order to emphasize how the ecology will be drastically changed, which will miraculously assist surviving humans with their personal economy. For instance, the river that I mentioned which will flow out from the temple on the temple mount in Jerusalem (Ezekiel 47:1) will flow with life-giving water.

*"Swarms of living creatures will live wherever the river flows. There will be large number of fish, because this water flows there and **makes the salt water fresh; so where the river flows everything will live**. Fishermen will stand along the shore; ...there will be places for spreading nets. **The fish will be of many kinds** – like the fish of the Great Sea. Fruit trees of all kinds will grow on both banks of the river. **Their leaves will not whither, nor will their fruit fail. Every month they will bear, because water from the sanctuary flows to them. Their fruit will serve for food and their leaves for healing"** (Ezekiel 47:9-10, 12 NIV).*

Please notice that you will witness a great miracle in which these rivers that emerge from the temple will be divine waters that change salt water to fresh water, heal the polluted waters to clean waters, have an over abundant supply of diverse fish, and will be a source of water to the miraculous trees growing along its banks. These trees will provide a harvest every month without fail and grow leaves that heal the sick. The river is medicinal and a tremendous source for fish and fruits for the population. And the beauty about this fish and fruit economy is that it will not cost anyone anything. *"Come all you who are thirsty, come to the waters; and you who have no money, come buy and eat! Come, buy wine and milk without money and without cost.* (Isaiah 55:1 NIV). It's all free! No one will be able to put a monopoly or ownership over God's heritage and bounty.

The abundance of rivers and waters are not limited to just the rivers flowing from the temple. After the great and terrible day of the Lord has destroyed all wickedness and evil, major cities and industries, and nations that opposed Jesus Christ, every mountain on earth will have streams of water providing nourishment to the survivors. *"In the day of the great slaughter, when the towers fall, streams of water will flow on every high mountain and every lofty hill"* (Isaiah 30:25 NIV). There will be no polluted or poisoned waters, nor will there be any waters that will contain parasites or microbes that can harm anyone.

Something else that is worthy of noting; as we see the river coming from the holy temple during the thousand years of Jesus' reign, so it shall be also in Heaven once everything has come to an end (see chapter four), where we also see a river flowing out of the throne of God. *"Then the angel showed me the river of the water of life, as clear as crystal, flowing from the throne of God and of the Lamb down the middle of the great street of the city. On each side of the river stood the tree of life, bearing twelve crops of fruit, yielding its fruit every month. And the leaves are for the healing of the nations"* (Revelation 22:1-2 NIV). Notice that the city of Jerusalem during the thousand years and the new city of Jerusalem in heaven has some commonalities: there is a great street or highway, there is a great river flowing from the throne of God as well as the temple on earth (Zechariah 13:1; Psalms 46:4), and there are trees yielding diverse fruit every month. There are songs that our churches sing that have lines that say: "Just like heaven on earth." Well in reality, the thousand years of Jesus reign will be so near perfect that it will be just like heaven on earth.

With an economy like this during the millennial years, you as a survivor will not have to worry about employment in order to acquire food and water. Sustenance will all be there for the taking for families, singles, aged, and children. There will be no need to fear for your safety, and because of the mass destruction of humankind, there will most likely be a lot of houses in which to live.

How will marriages and families
change during the new world order?

Marriage and bearing children will be reserved to the surviving mortals upon the earth as yourself, and not the immortals who were raptured and returned to the earth to reign with Jesus for the thousand years. The immortals will not be fleshly beings but spirit beings. They will have spiritual bodies just like the glorified body of Jesus Christ. *"Who by the power that enables him to bring everything under His control, will transform our lowly bodies so that they will be like His glorious body"* (Philippians 3:21 NIV). The immortals will not be given in marriage nor will they bear children, but will be much like the angels of Heaven (Matthew 22:30).

As I mentioned before, not many males will survive the great tribulation, the battle of Armageddon, or the vengeful second coming of Jesus Christ. *"I will **make man scarcer than pure gold**, more rare than the gold of Ophir"* (Isaiah 13:12 NIV). Isaiah reiterates the rarity of men surviving. *"Therefore a curse consumes the earth; its people must bear their guilt. Therefore earth's inhabitants are burned up, **and very few are left"*** (Isaiah 24:6 NIV). So you might imagine that once the dust of the second coming settles, there will be very few survivors, and the vast majority of the survivors will be women. As an example, a town of one hundred people may have just one man remaining, and he may be the sole survivor of the war, or the only one left behind in the rapture.

With very few males alive and available, women will discover it quite difficult to find a man to marry, establish a family, and bear children. The frustration of the women without men to build a family with, in any given township, will bring them to negotiate, possibly, with already married men. *"In that day seven women will take hold of one man and say, 'We will eat our own food and provide our own clothes; only let us be called by your name. Take away our disgrace!'"* (Isaiah 4:1 NIV)

The literal new world order of Jesus Christ will bring about the fulfillment of the prayer Jesus taught us in the "Our Father," which includes the words: "Thy Kingdom come, Thy will be done, on earth as it is in heaven." The great changes that will come with Jesus' new world reign will be the establishment of a world that is an all-inclusive God-fearing earth. And though the millennial kingdom will not be the culmination of all things, the new world order will certainly set straight all the governments of the world under the sole authority of Jesus Christ who is the King of all kings, and the Lord of all lords upon the earth.

A LUCID DREAM OF MINE

Some years ago, I experienced a dream that was certainly from the Lord. Please know that it isn't very common for me to dream such spiritually lucid dreams; I have had fewer than a handful in my entire life (that I know of). In the dream I was witnessing the conditions of a remote village during the millennial reign. Because this dream occurred years ago, I did not know it was the millennium, for at that time I hadn't been given the information I am sharing in this book.

In the dream, I found myself in a village with not-so-nicely clothed townspeople living in a few communal houses with army cot-like beds, and army surplus green blankets on the beds.

Everyone seemed pleasant enough, but they were very busy preparing for a great visitation to their community. I did not know who was coming to their town, but they were preparing by cleaning up, tidying up their homes, and setting aside some long, plastic beaded necklaces as gifts for their visitors. I recall walking into one of their homes where there were a few beds with about a dozen or so of these necklaces carefully placed on them. I noticed a man with a clipboard, who was evidently a leader, ensuring that everything was being organized properly. He had a slightly shabby, long blue coat, similar to what a doorman wears, or a dress-blue military coat with a uniform round hat. I noticed that the long coat he wore had a small hole in the sleeve on the left side near his shoulder. He never spoke, but I recognized him from a church I once attended.

When I stepped outside again, I saw a man with a construction tool building a short wall of large rocks around the house. He appeared to look like my biological father, who had passed away when he was only thirty-eight years old from an aneurysm. Strangely, the man was using snow as mortar or cement to hold the stones in place–evidently taken from the patches of frost on the ground. I waved to him and he smiled and waved back.

My curiosity brought me to ask a man who happened to be briskly walking by, "Who are you all getting ready to receive? Who is coming?" He stopped and said that it was a procession coming through with the raptured saints of God, and that they were beside themselves with great anticipation and joy. I had to ask the second question as to why they were so excited about them parading through their hometown. Strangely, he leaned in toward me with a huge smile and scratched through his hair rigorously until a small cloud of white particles that looked like dandruff burst forth. As he continued to smile at me, I said I didn't understand. To that end he said but one word, "Stories!"

I totally understood at that point. The raptured people have the benefit of seeing heaven, being with Jesus Christ closely, and fellowshipping with angels from heaven. They had wonderful stories to share with those communities that did not have the opportunity to see what the elect could see, and could educate them as well as inform them of the times.

After speaking with this man, I looked over to the man who looked like my dad that I saw building the exterior wall. He had finished an incredible amount of work in that short time. It appeared that his wall was over a football field's length away from where I saw him just minutes before. I knew I was not a resident there, but merely a witness of something I have come to believe was a microcosmic vision of the conditions of a common village on the earth after the second coming. These townspeople were either not raptured, or they were born on the earth during the millennial.

Through the years, I also concluded that raptured people, and even Jews who worked as priests in the temple, were highly sought after individuals, for they were a tremendous blessing to all that they visited or taught. I was also overtaken by the unified joy and anticipation of everyone, and how deliberate they were to prepare for and please these highly honored guests. I also noticed that everyone seemed to have all things in common. I don't think there was any form of currency, but more of a sharing and bartering system. Because of what I now know of the thousand-year conditions, I understand that work and labor was a pleasure and without great strain, and that plants, fruits, and vegetables grew inordinately quick, and that there was no need for fear of their security. I envisioned this place as a small example of peace and calm in the entire community. I also didn't see any reason to work outside of gardening and farming. The man with the clipboard seemed to be an assigned person that insured that all the loose ends were tied and nothing was ignored or forgotten.

I never actually saw the arrival of the procession of the raptured people; I came out of my dream with a lot of questions that would only be answered once I received this revelation of the kingdom that I am sharing with you now. The new world order will be an amazing environment for the survivors, to be sure, for they will be blessed beyond any experience they have ever had. Their love for God and the people will be the order of the day rather than the exception. Although eventually some will rebel, this village I had the pleasure to visit in a dream was indeed, a very inviting and loving place to be. And I suspect that most will share the same sentiment.

I presently could not imagine even a small village on the earth right now that would outshine the love of God as the one I witnessed in my vision. Imagine the city in which you live, where all the people were open with their Christianity. Or imagine a town where everyone is a strong, practicing Christian, without exception. What a wonderful environment that would be. However, with Jesus upon the earth as the King of all kings, the entire world will be Christian, and no lying doctrines or cults or atheism will be found. How pleasant the world will be for those thousand years.

Chapter Three

Ezekiel's Perfect Millennial Temple: Where Jesus Reigns

"But I say unto you, swear not at all; neither by heaven; for it is God's throne; nor by earth; for it is His footstool; neither by Jerusalem; for it is the City of the Great King."
(Matthew 5:34-35 KJV)

In this chapter you will find details of the Jewish temple that will be built in Jerusalem during the thousand years, specifically positioned on the old temple mount. It is vital that you know about this temple as a survivor, because it will become your center of everything—from Law to policies, from religious ceremonies to mandatory visitations. The temple will actually become much like the United States' Washington, D.C., No. 10 Downing Street of London, England, the Kremlin of Russia, the Tiananmen Square of China, and the Mecca of Saudi Arabia, in so many ways. The King of kings will reside and work from the temple, annual feasts will be hosted there, and all the major teachings will be heralded from Jesus in and around the temple area as well. If you wanted to see Jesus Christ (just typing those words seems so surreal) you will quickly locate Him at this very temple.

As you will discover in this chapter, Jesus Christ will reinstitute animal sacrifice, which will be very important to you as a survivor and your relationship with the King. A survivor will be expected to participate regularly by way of viewing the annual Feast of Tabernacles and to study the reason for the temple layout and the furniture within each of the numerous rooms. Many priests and Levites (temple workers) will be there throughout the day, and you will be led to ask many questions concerning the importance of the different temple instruments and equipment used by the priests in order to perform their respective ministrations. It may not seem that important to you right now, but you will find that the temple and all of its activities are crucial to your life on the earth. This will determine whether or not you will have a pleasant and blessed experience or a short-lived difficult experience on earth and in the final judgment. My point to you is–everything surrounds this temple. Everything.

You will find that the temple in Jerusalem is by far the most prominent center in Jesus' worldwide government during the millennial period. Jesus will reign from the great City of Jerusalem over the entire earth right from His throne, which is situated in the Temple; and to be more specific–directly from the Holy of Holies (Zechariah 6:13). Jesus will use this holy temple as the governmental center of the world, which will be the Capitol of the earth. I could refer the place where Jesus will sit in the holiest of holies as a type of Oval Office, but that would be incorrect. His abode is a throne room like no human has ever seen, or like any sitting king or pharaoh ever had the pleasure to sit upon.

The temple is precisely described by Ezekiel and will be quite different from all previous temples and the tabernacle in the wilderness. Almost everything about the size, dimensions, the furniture, the designed structure, and even purpose, will stand in contrast to the other temple structures. Also, Ezekiel's temple should not be mistaken for the rebuilt temple, which Christians are now watching and waiting for in these last days. Ezekiel's temple will be erected after the second coming and will be void of the Antichrist and false prophet or any wicked presence and influence. This is actually the long-awaited temple that the Jewish people have been longing for many centuries. This is the perfect temple.

The Jews have been waiting for their Messiah who will reign with a mighty scepter, destroy their enemies, rebuild Israel, and restore His people. The Jews are also eagerly awaiting the reinstitution of the temple along with animal sacrifice. Presently, there are Jewish organizations that are attempting to prepare for the rebuilt temple in Jerusalem along with animal sacrifice. However, the temple Israel is hoping to build is not the same temple that Ezekiel is referring to. Ezekiel's temple will be a temple for all surviving humans on the earth after the second coming of Jesus Christ, no matter their nationality, or whether they are Gentile or Jew. This temple will be the centerpiece of every human survivor by way of religion, government, health, welfare, and their spiritual future.

The millennial temple is prophesied to be massive

Ezekiel describes a temple that will dwarf all of the previous temples and the tabernacle in the wilderness. This temple will span over one-and-one-quarter city blocks, and will be surrounded by a nine-foot wall. The temple property will stretch three-and-one-half miles square. Ezekiel's temple will have three stories, with thirty rooms designated for temple equipment, choir instruments, rooms for priests and Levites, and butchery rooms for slaughtered sacrificial animals. Ezekiel chapter four provides the reader with the most minute of details of this temple edifice. There are actually more details of Ezekiel's temple through his book (see Ezekiel chapters 41, 42, 45) than the details of all other prior temples and tabernacle put together. The massiveness of this temple (which also includes other buildings on the temple grounds) is to receive all of the nations of the world that come annually in order to worship the King and honor the Feast of Tabernacles. This will be an annual pilgrimage for all surviving mankind to show homage to Jesus Christ and His Lordship at the temple located on the temple mount, which will become miraculously the highest point in Jerusalem. Presently, it is not.

WHY WILL JESUS RESTORE
ANIMAL SACRIFICE?

During the millennium, there will be sacrifices on a regular basis in addition to the three Levitical Feasts: Passover (of bulls and goats, but interestingly not lambs), The Feast of Unleavened Bread, and the Feast of Tabernacles. The millennial feasts are detailed in Ezekiel 45:13–46:15.

This portion of the tabernacle's description may be difficult for some readers to initially accept, because like me, I have learned that Jesus was and is the ultimate sacrifice for sins and that there would be no need for animal sacrifice after He bled on the cross for all of mankind (Hebrews 10:12-18). But Ezekiel, a priest in his own right, is seemingly delighted with sacrificial restoration. Why is Ezekiel so delighted with this restoration? Ezekiel made it regretfully clear that the Holy Spirit had departed from the temple and Israel in his day (Ezekiel 11:23), but His Spirit would return to the temple and Israel (Ezekiel 43:1-2, 44:2-3) during the reign of Jesus Christ and recognize the sacrifices that lay on the brazen altar as memorials of what Jesus did for all of mankind.

The reinstitution of animal sacrifice in the temple during the thousand-year reign of Jesus Christ is not debated among a myriad of commentaries; there is no controversy among pre-millennialists that believe in a literal animal sacrificial system for the thousand years (with the exception of the amillennialists as mentioned in Appendix B). The struggle is not the reinstitution of animal sacrifice. The struggle remains as to why animal sacrifice is reinstituted when Jesus' blood trumps all animal sacrifices.

First, the reinstitution of animal sacrifices is not for the washing away of our sins, because animal sacrifice has never had the power to wash away our sins. What Old Testament animal sacrifices did accomplish was to point us **toward the cross** as a type and shadow or an example of atonement. And animal sacrifice in the millennial reign will point mankind **back to the cross** as an example and more specifically—a reminder—of what Jesus did for us on the cross as a living sacrifice. Animal sacrifice has always served us as an educational illustration of the cross, and animal sacrifice will serve as an educational illustration for those who are born during the millennium as well.

You will find this advantageous as a survivor because foreigners (or Gentiles) will be given the opportunity to bring an animal sacrifice to the temple as well. This is very unique, because non-Jewish people have never been able to offer animal offerings (or even walk into the temple area, for that matter). Gentiles were considered (and are considered) unclean in the eyes of the ultra-conservative Hasidic Jew. Only Jewish people had the right to offer a sacrifice on the holy altar of God. But during the millennial, all of mankind, Jew and Gentile, will be given this opportunity if they love His name, obey His ordinances, and are found to be in covenant with Jesus Christ. *"And the foreigners who bind themselves to the Lord to serve Him, to love the name of the Lord, and to worship Him, all who keep the Sabbath without desecrating it and hold fast to my covenant – these I will bring to my holy mountain and give them joy in my house of prayer. **Their burnt offers and sacrifices will be accepted upon my altar; for my house will be called a house of prayer for all*** *nations. The Sovereign Lord declares – He who gathers the exiles of Israel: I will gather still others to them besides those already gathered"* (Isaiah 56:6-8 NIV).

Survivors will come to the annual celebration and pilgrimage for the Feast of Tabernacles (Zechariah 14:16).

ONLY THE SEED OF ZADOK WILL BE ALLOWED TO PERFORM ANIMAL SACRIFICE

Selected priests of the temple will make these animal sacrifices. Not all of the Hebrews that are in the bloodline of Aaron's priesthood will be chosen to be a part of the holy rituals of animal sacrifices during the millennium because of their abominable sins of the past that God cannot ignore. Only the seed (descendants) of the holy priest Zadok will be selected by Jesus Christ to conduct all of the ministrations of the temple as priests, *"They are not to come near to serve me as priests or come near any of my holy things or my most holy offerings; they must bear the shame of their detestable practices. Yet will I put them in charge of the duties of the temple and all the work that is to be done in it. But the priests who are Levites and descendants of Zadok and who faithfully carried out the duties of my sanctuary when the Israelites went astray from me, are to come near to minister before me; they are to stand before me to offer sacrifices of fat and blood, declares the Sovereign Lord. They alone are to enter my sanctuary; they alone are to come near my table to minister before me and perform my service"* (Ezekiel 44:13-16 NIV).

The Almighty God has kept a record of all of His holy priests. He has always expected much more from His ministers than He has with the general population. Priests must stand before God and give an account of their service to Him and to His people, and there are serious consequences for those who have enjoyed the benefits of ministry without accepting the commitment or responsibility that comes with the office. The sons of Zadok alone have emerged from the fray of their sinful brothers, and are blessed for his faithfulness.

The reasoning for the function of animal sacrifice in Ezekiel's temple is considered one of the most difficult portions of Scripture in the entire Bible–even for the Messianic Jews. Many commentaries, both ancient and modern, have found themselves at a loss as to what to make of these post-resurrection sacrifices. The commentary of Matthew Henry has provided some good wisdom in this regard. He writes: "Faith accepts God's word as it is, waits for the event, and will clear up all such difficulties."

To further help you rationalize the reinstitution of animal sacrifice, let me remind you that the marriage supper of the Lamb is just that – *of the Lamb*. Jesus displays Himself at this supper as a person of no reputation, not even as the Lion of the tribe of Judah—which He is. Jesus chooses to show Himself to His Bride as *the Lamb* at the supper, and not as the ferocious returning King of Kings, or even the transfigured Christ in all of His glory. The figure of the Lamb is the fullest display of His Love. The Lamb is the fullest expression of His character. The Bride will see Him manifested in what represents the reason for our total salvation and why we are present in the marriage supper in the first place. I also believe that Jesus delights in the showing Himself to us as the Lamb, because it is the culmination of all of His sufferings and sacrifice for us all. And this is the reason that of all the sacrifices that will be made during the thousand years (oxen, goats, and sheep), there will not be another lamb sacrificed. Those who reject Jesus actually are rejecting the Lamb in all of His sufferings. They virtually disown the slaughtered *Lamb of God*. Those who reject, disown, or have a lack of appreciation or love for the Lamb will not be invited to the marriage supper.

This is why I believe there will be a continuance of sacrifices in order to reaffirm what the Lamb of God did for all of us. As I mentioned previously, animal sacrifices in the Old

Testament pointed to the cross, and during the millennial, animal sacrifices will point back to the cross. And though Jesus will not appear as the Lamb in the Temple, there will be blood sacrifices constantly relating the Lamb of God to the animals being sacrificed. The world doesn't know the Lamb of God or the tremendous slaughter He underwent for us. However, this lesson will be continually taught to the surviving humans on the earth and to their offspring for a thousand years. He was the Lamb led to slaughter, and the temple and animal sacrifice will be the continuous reminder of that.

There will not be any casual onlookers of the animal sacrifices or those who have no appreciation for Him. This is the reason God will curse by withholding rain to any nation that refuses to annually travel to the temple to celebrate the Feast of Tabernacles, which incidentally will involve animal sacrifice. The lack of attendance is interpreted as the lack of love toward the Lamb and the horrific ordeal He experienced as the slaughtered Lamb.

There are five specific animal sacrifices that are made to God, which are for sin, trespass, thanksgiving, guilt, and fellowship. And of these specific offerings, the priests of Zadok's pure bloodline will offer them to God during the Feast of Tabernacles. And once again, these offerings all point to the crucifixion and sacrifice of the Lamb of God that came to take away the sins of the world.

Paul was resolute when He told the Corinthians, *"For I resolved to know nothing while I was with you except Jesus Christ and **Him crucified**"* (1 Corinthians 2:2 NIV). He also told the Philippians, *"I want to know Christ—yes, to know the power of His resurrection and **participation in His sufferings, becoming like Him in His death*** (Philippians 3:10 NIV). There should never be a time that we forget what He has done for us as the Lamb, and I see that the sacrifices at the temple ensures that mankind will not forget.

When Jesus told His disciples at the last supper as He broke the bread, "And He took bread, gave thanks and broke it, and gave it to them, saying, this is my body given to you; do this in remembrance of Me" (Luke 22:19 NIV). Jesus was actually referring to more than the bread, but also the Passover lamb that was just eaten by all that sat at the table during the Passover feast. He was insistent that we always remember the example of the Lamb that was to be led to slaughter. And this example will not be forgotten during the millennial kingdom either.

In Revelation 5:6 (NIV), Jesus remained depicted to the Apostle John as a slain Lamb, even after His ascension, ***"Then I saw a Lamb, looking as if it had been slain***, *standing at the center of the throne, encircled by the four living creatures and the elders. The Lamb had seven horns and seven eyes, which are the seven spirits of God sent out to all the earth."* Jesus retains the marks of His past deadly wounds, standing at the most prominent place in heaven— the throne of God and before the twenty-four elders. Christ crucified will be the prominent theme of the temple during His thousand-year reign. There will be the continued efficacy of His sin-cleansing blood, who is the Lamb slain from the foundation of the world.

Saints under the altar in heaven

In Revelation 6:9, John the revelator saw the souls of the martyrs under the altar, at the foot of the altar in heaven, which is at the feet of Jesus Christ. These were those who remained faithful to Him even in death and their ultimate sacrifice of themselves. These are those who did not recant Christ nor deny Him in hopes of saving their own lives. These are those who have found a restful place from their earthly labors, though longing for their avenging by the King of Kings and Lord of Lords. They emulate Paul the apostle who said, *"For I am now ready to be offered, and the time of my departure is at hand"* (2 Timothy 4:6

KJV). Tertullian stated, "The souls of martyrs repose in peace under the altar, and cherish a spirit of patience until others are admitted to fill up their communion glow." The church father Irenaeus said of them, "The souls of the departed go to a place assigned to them by God, and there abide until the resurrection, when they will be united to their bodies; and then the saints, both in soul and body, will come into the presence of God." The Gill's expository states that the phrase "the souls of them that are slain" is actually a Jewish term, for they believe that souls of those who are slain are kept in certain palaces, under the care of one appointed by God, and these were seen *under the altar.* Either this is said in allusion to the blood of the sacrifices, which is poured out from the bottom of the altar (Leviticus 4:7), or because martyrdom is a sacrifice of men's lives, for the souls of the righteous are treasured up under the throne of God. It is possible however, that the term "under the altar" may mean "under Jesus Christ," enjoying communion with Him, in whose hands they committed their souls unto death.

No matter how a reader looks at this, the picture of one under the altar certainly represents the blood of a sacrificed victim on the altar, which was poured at the bottom of the altar. These slain, lying beneath the altar, are shut up unto Him in joyful eager expectancy of their resurrection.

Where are all the missing pieces of furniture in the temple?

Within the previous Jewish temples and the tabernacle in the wilderness, there were certain pieces of furniture that symbolically represented and pointed to Jesus Christ. These pieces of furniture, through function and ritual, all had very important messages to New Testament readers of the coming salvation of Jesus. But in Ezekiel's detailed description of the millennial temple, there are certain pieces of furniture missing, and much of the reason for the absence of certain furniture is the literal physical presence of Jesus Christ. What need is there to have a type and shadow of His presence if His presence is genuinely manifested?

Never a mention of any gold in the temple

Ironically, as beautiful and perfect as the temple is described by Ezekiel, there is no mention of any gold found anywhere in the temple. To give you a stark comparison of Ezekiel's temple from Solomon's temple, Solomon accumulated over 3,000 tons of gold throughout the inner rooms. The Table of Shew Bread was made of gold, as was the Altar of Incense, and the candlesticks (Menorah).

Even the candle implements were made of gold, as was the fire tongs, the basins, the snuffers, and fire-pans—all of them were made of pure beaten gold. The doors were equipped with gold hinges. The inner sanctuary was elaborately covered with gold, and the holy place displayed gold chains across the front entrance.

Evidently, the central value of Ezekiel's temple is found in the presence of Jesus Christ and not in gold. Everyone, including the human survivors, will find the beauty and majesty of Jesus Christ far more valuable than gold, silver, or precious stones. *"And the government shall be on His shoulders. He will be called **wonderful** counselor, Mighty God, Everlasting Father, Prince of Peace"* (Isaiah 9:6 KJV). Isaiah captures the essence of His wonder, majesty and beauty, which is found in the glory of His presence.

Ark of the Covenant is not present in the holy of holies

The Ark was a chest-like piece of furniture. I liken it unto a piece of luggage that carried the covenant or Ten Commandments, the jar of manna, and Aaron's rod or walking staff. But it was more than a piece of luggage; it had a "mercy seat" affixed on its top that served as a place where God manifested Himself for the purpose of providing mercy and atonement. The Ark is a symbol of Jesus Christ where God meets the sinner through Him.

In Ezekiel's temple, the Ark of the Covenant will be replaced with Jesus Himself, for He is the presence of the Almighty God. Jesus will be found sitting upon David's throne as the true propitiation for sin, living in the temple among His people, the Jews. *"He said son of man, this is the place of my throne and the place for the soles of my feet. This is where I will live among the Israelites..."* (Ezekiel 43:7 NIV). This is amazing in that Jesus Christ can physically be found on His throne, and not for just a few days, months, or years, but for one thousand years! Everyone will look at Him in all of His glory, and not a symbolic wooden box (ark) that merely represents Him.

The veil is gone

You might recall when Jesus died on the cross, that immediately the thick veil in the temple of Jerusalem (some two thousand years ago) ripped from top to bottom (Matthew 27:51). This act of God was indicative to opening the holiest of holies to everyone, not just to the priests. The approach to God no longer required a high priest to represent us; we now can personally come boldly before the throne of grace (Hebrews 4:16). And the ripping was to proclaim that there would be no separation of the people from the Ark of the Covenant, which was a symbol of Jesus Christ. With the veil removed, we can personally come before the Lord without any barriers. It is the expression of grace and mercy that is instituted through the death of the Lamb of God.

The veil that separated the holy place from the holy of holies is not present in Ezekiel's temple description. Instead of a veil, Ezekiel describes a wood paneled wall with one double wooden door that separates the holy place and the holy of holies, which is now the throne room of King Jesus. On one of the doors there is an etched picture of a face of a man, and on the other door – a face of a lion. This is indicative to the relationship between man and the Lion of the Tribe of Judah, Jesus Christ.

The wall of partition is removed

It has always been the Jewish law and custom to separate men and women in public assemblies, especially in the temple. So if you happen to be a female survivor, you will not be segregated from the men during assembles in Ezekiel's temple. The Hebrew word *Mechitza* refers to the physical divider that was placed between the men and women's section in the temple. The Bible refers to the different courts or sections of the temple such as the outer court, the court of the Gentiles and the women's court. The women's section of the temple in Hebrew is called *Erat Nashim.* Though most reformed Jews do not recognize the separation of the genders, the orthodox and the Hasidic certainly do. In 2013, I had the privilege to visit the Wailing Wall in Jerusalem. There I noticed that a partition separated the men from the women. The men certainly had the lion's share of the wall, leaving a small remaining section for the women. I also noticed that many Jewish orthodox prayer groups, public rituals, and celebrations (in the form of small parades) in Jerusalem were made up of only men. The wall of partition in Ezekiel's temple that separates men and women isn't there. Evidently, the need to divide the two genders is not important during the reign of Jesus Christ. Paul tells the Galatian church, *"There is neither Jew nor Gentile, neither slave nor free, **nor is there male and female**, for you are all one in Christ Jesus"* (Galatians 3:28 KJV). Approaching the King of Kings within the temple requires no gender distinction. Formerly, females were not admitted to the sacred rites and holy ceremonies that males so freely enjoyed. But under the new world order of Jesus Christ there is no wall or barrier to delineate the sexes from the divine things of God.

The bronze laver is gone

The bronze laver was a huge water basin set in front of the temple for the purpose of washing and cleansing the priests, and only the priests, from defilement. A priests, before he could enter the temple, had to wash his hands and feet. *"For Aaron and his sons shall wash their hands and their feet in water from it. When they go into the tabernacle of meeting, or when they come near the altar to minister, to burn an offering made by fire to the LORD, they shall wash with water, lest they die"* (Exodus 30:19-20 KJV). As serious as the washing of the hands and feet of the priests were according to the temple laws, Ezekiel's temple does not include the bronze laver. The ritual washing of the hands and feet of the priests falls far short of the cleansing from Jesus Christ's blood, which washes not only on the outside of the body, but on the inside as well, which is far more relevant.

The golden lampstand is not mentioned

In the temple, the golden lampstand was positioned in the holy place. The physical purpose of the lamp was to provide light in the temple day and night (Exodus 27:20-21). It was actually the only source of light in the temple that was permitted. The golden lampstand is missing in Ezekiel's temple. The lampstand is actually a type and shadow of the light the Holy Spirit sheds upon us and that Jesus Christ is the light of the world. The light is intended to take His children out of darkness into His marvelous light (1 Peter 2:9). But with Jesus physically present to shed light on all things, then there is no need for the symbolism the lampstand represents.

The table of showbread isn't there

The purpose of the golden table of showbread was to hold twelve cakes of bread made of fine flour. They were placed on two rows of six, each loaf representing one of the tribes of Israel (Leviticus 24:8). The term showbread or showbread literally means "the bread of face," or the bread set before the face or presence of God.

The table of showbread not present in Ezekiel's description of the temple because Jesus is the bread of life, and He is present. The body may be sustained by bread, but the soul is alive from the Word of God. The satisfying of a man's hunger runs far deeper than the physical hunger he may experience. A spiritually healthy man cannot be sustained with mere bread, but the presence of the Son of God, speaking the word of God, that will sustain him. The nature of the physical bread provides nutrition to the body, and the spiritual emphasis is to provide nutrition to the soul.

The altar of incense is removed

The altar of incense isn't found within Ezekiel's temple either. This altar of incense stood between the holy of holies and the holy place, just in front of the veil. The altar served as a place of offering of sweet fragrant incense to God—as a form of prayer to God. The incense was a mixture of three spices that were blended together and beaten into a fine powder and with salt added as well. It was totally forbidden for this mixture of spices to be used for any other reason than for the worship of God in the holy place. The incense was poured upon the hot coals of this altar, which gave forth a delightful aroma, which was likened to quality prayer to God. In the millennium, with Jesus receiving all the praise and worship, there will be no need for an altar of incense to Him.

The physical presence of Jesus Christ in the temple provides all truth of the knowledge of God. *"For the earth will be filled with the knowledge of the glory of the Lord, as the waters cover the sea"* (Habakkuk 2:14 KJV). And everyone will know the truth about Jesus Christ, for Jesus Himself will teach all the surviving nations from His throne in the temple. *"Many nations will come and say, let us go up to the mountain of the Lord, to the house of God of Jacob. He will teach us His ways, so that we may walk in His paths. The Law will go out from Zion, the word of the Lord from Jerusalem"* (Micah 4:2 NIV). These teaching would include the Ten Commandments, the Torah, His ordinances and laws, sacrifices, His character, the prophecies written of Him, and the future eternity with God Almighty.

I cannot emphasize how very important this temple, as meticulously described by Ezekiel, will be. The very idea that the temple serves as a type of "White House" for all the world, and Jerusalem, could be likened unto the Washington DC of the world for the thousand years. I cannot imagine a world where every nation will be Christian and every law will have a religious foundation enforced by Jesus Christ, who will be the ruler of the entire world.

Every element of Jesus' policies will be grounded by what takes place in this perfect temple. Every law, custom, governance, theology, and personal responsibility will be taught and emphasized from this amazing temple of Jesus Christ. Jesus Christ will provide all instruction, every biblical lesson, and every Scripture interpretation. His words are absolute, and not open for others' opinions or different points of view. All things will be made crystal clear to you as a blessed human survivor, and you must accept every word that proceeds out of His mouth without question.

The temple proclaiming
the perpetual Jubilee

The key and longed-for announcement among the people of God is to hear, coming from the temple, the high priest sounding the *shofar* indicating the beginning of the Jubilee.

Every fifty years God instructed the priests to sound the ram's horns to proclaim the year of Jubilee, which was a year that all debts were absolved, all properties and land returned to the original owner, all slaves were released to their own families, and liberty was proclaimed throughout the land. Though this was a wonderful time for those who were needy, the Jewish nobles didn't observe Sabbath years or Jubilees very often because it meant they had to return land that they acquired and slaves that they ruled over.

When Jesus, during His earthly ministry, approached the temple pulpit, He chose to read from Isaiah 61:1-3, which clearly is a description of how wonderful things will be for the inhabitants of the earth during the millennial kingdom. What He was virtually saying was there is a jubilee coming to the earth that will be eternal for all people who believe in Him. Isaiah's prophecy read: *"The Spirit of the Lord is upon Me, because He has anointed Me to preach good news to the poor. He has sent Me to proclaim freedom for the prisoners and recovery of sight to the blind, to release the oppressed, to proclaim the year of the Lord's favor"* (Luke 4:18-19 KJV) And then Jesus closes with, what the priests interpreted as blasphemy, *"Today this scripture is fulfilled in your hearing"* (Luke 4:21). However, when you refer to the actual verses of Isaiah 61, you will see a lot more that Jesus will have to offer: ***"And the day of vengeance of our God"*** (Isaiah 61:2 KJV). Actually, although Jesus said this prophecy has been fulfilled by His presence on earth, a few of these Scriptures in Isaiah 61:1-11 haven't been fulfilled, such as God avenging the earth, or the rebuilding of the ancient ruins as the temple. Clearly, Isaiah is referring to the thousand-year reign of Christ and His second coming.

Also, when Jesus said that He was proclaiming the year of the Lord's favor, He was referring once again to how well He will treat the people on the earth—much like He did during a recognized year of jubilee. But, in the case of the millennial reign, there will be no need any longer for *seasons* of blessings, because there will be an eternal jubilee without a beginning or an ending. The earth will not need a rest because the land will be "Eden-like," which is a God-blessed soil, incapable of depreciation.

God had told the Hebrews that every sabbatical year and every jubilee they were not to till, plow, or fertilize the earth. God told them that, during the year of jubilee or a sabbatical year, the land needed a rest of all plowing, fertilizing, and harvesting. So when the people refused to honor these holy years, God arranged for an exile to forcibly pull the Israelites out of the land, and by removing the people from Israel, the land thereby received the needed rest (2 Chronicles 36:20-21). And by having the nobles put under the power of the Babylonians and the Assyrians, they were now enslaved because they refused to release their slaves during the sabbatical years and jubilees. When Daniel prayed an intercessory prayer to God for his personal sins and the sins of Israel, Gabriel answered with a jubilee timeline starting at the restoration of the temple to the jubilee at the time of Christ's crucifixion. Then Gabriel continues and states that there will be a remaining seventy jubilees that the temple and all Israel can enjoy until the second coming. Some commentaries believe that the last jubilee will be completed either during the 2015-2016, 2016-2017, or the year 2017-2018. No one knows for sure when the next jubilee will be because of the confusion between the Jewish and the Gregorian calendars. However, Daniel is very particular that there is a final jubilee, which is the seventieth after the death of the Christ (Daniel 9:20-27).

Why is the end of a seasonal jubilee important, especially where the temple is concerned? Because it will also mark the finishing of all transgression, the putting away and the end of sin, the atonement of iniquity, the bringing in of everlasting righteousness, the establishment of the most holy place (the most inner chamber of the temple), and the arrival of the Anointed One (Daniel 9:24). This marks the perpetual reestablishment of dealing directly with temple sacrifice and the mercy of King Jesus, who will be located within the holiest of holies. Also, during the millennium, there will be no further use of a jubilee in order to return all of one's property, or to release those who are enslaved, because once again, the jubilee will be heralded by the priests with ram's horns for the perpetuity of jubilee!

THE TREE OF LIFE IS TRANSPLANTED
TO THE TEMPLE

Do you recall the tree of life in Genesis 2:9? This tree gave all kinds of beautiful and attractive fruit in the Garden of Eden during the days of Adam and Eve. As a matter of fact, it gave them the ability to live a long life. They actually could have lived forever had the angels not cast them out of the garden and stood guard at the entry way of the garden to block any attempts of Adam or his family to return to eat from the tree of life (Genesis 3:22). Because of their sin and fall from grace, Adam and Eve had a sentence of eventual death placed upon them. This is a huge reason for you to become knowledgeable of the temple grounds, because the actual tree of life will be relocated from heaven and planted right within the temple grounds. Those who are allowed to eat from this tree will live forever. The tree will not be available until after Jesus has invaded the earth and destroyed all wickedness and evil. Then it will become available to mortal survivors just like you!

*"And as for this fragrant tree **no mortal is permitted to touch it till the great judgment**, when He shall take vengeance on all and bring everything to its consummation for ever. It shall then be given to the righteous and holy. Its fruit shall be for food to the elect: **it shall be transplanted to the holy place, to the temple of the Lord, the Eternal King.** Then they shall rejoice with joy and be glad. And into the holy place shall they enter; and its fragrance shall be in their bones, and they shall live a long life on earth, such as thy fathers lived: and in their days shall be no sorrow or plague or torment or calamity touches them. Then blessed I the God of Glory, the Eternal King, who hath prepared such things for the righteous, and hath created them and promised to give to them."* (Enoch 25:4-7)

Did you notice that the very fragrance of the tree will be in and on those who eat from it? The scent of the tree of life will be the perfume or cologne of those who are permitted to partake of it; everyone will know you are a partaker of the tree of life just by the aroma you will give off. When Adam and Eve gazed upon this tree at the time of mankind's infancy, they made mention that the tree was beautiful to look at and the fruit that grew upon it looked delicious. So it will be for you and all the survivors of the earth. The tree of life will appear as a most wondrous and beautiful sight of delicious and diverse fruits for you to eat.

THE BUILDING OF A HOLY HIGHWAY TO THE TEMPLE

*"**And an highway shall be there**, and a way, and it shall be called the way to holiness; the unclean shall not pass over it; but it shall be for those: the wayfaring men, though fools, shall not err therein"* (Isaiah 35:8 KJV). This highway in which Isaiah refers to could be taken strictly symbolically, or it may have a duel implication; it may well be a literal highway.

Symbolically, this holy concourse can be seen, for instance, as a pathway of truth, godliness, and holiness –thus, the Holy Highway. It is the symbolism of a direct road to Christ, which will be made plain, and it will be a safe journey to Him, free from all deception and opposition. There will not be a Satan or unclean demon to contend with to disorient a seeker. There will not be any misunderstanding as to the direction of this straight road to truth, for it will be well marked with many seekers of truth travelling upon it. Isaiah alludes that the way will be clearly heralded to all of the survivors upon the earth, *"And thine ears shall hear a word behind thee, saying, This is the way, walk ye in it, when ye turn to the right hand, and when ye turn to the left"* (Isaiah 30:21 KJV). Doubtlessly, a survivor will not miss the truth.

However, I am inclined to believe personally that this reference of Isaiah will be a literal highway as well. For this highway shall be a raised up and elevated highway to the throne of King Jesus which is in the holy temple. The highway will be virtually impossible not to spot by any wayfarer. I see a physical fulfillment of the prophecy spoken of John the Baptist, when Isaiah said, *"A voice of one calling: In the desert prepare the way of the Lord; make straight in the wilderness a highway of our God. Every valley shall be raised up, **every mountain and hill made low; the rough ground shall become level, the rugged places made plain**. And the glory of the Lord shall be revealed, and all mankind together will see it. For the mouth of the Lord has spoken"* (Isaiah 40:3-5 NIV).

I realize that this was a symbolic revelation, prophesying the voice of John the Baptist crying in the wilderness, preparing the way of Jesus Christ. But I believe there is a dual revelation here, actually fulfilling the prophecy that all of mankind shall see Him (Isaiah 40:5). When a city prepares to build a highway, mountains are often cut into or leveled, hills are removed, and valleys are filled in. I see a real highway that will allow the nations to journey more simply to the temple and to the throne of God without obstructions and impediments that could block the passage to Him. The annual pilgrimage, for instance, in which all nations are to travel to the temple each year, can amount to millions of men, women, and children of all ages. The passage to get to the temple must be easily passable for everyone, no matter their age or physical condition.

Also, I see this highway as literal because it is not uncommon for the capital of a nation to have a causeway, Broadway, or highway that is made especially for the king—thus, a King's Highway, if you will. These highways are often very aesthetically pleasing and adorned with signs, memorials, and statutes along the way in recognition of the city and her leader. These King's Highways are often used for patriotic parades, marching armies displaying flags that signify their allegiance, and also to honor a person much like a ticker tape parade through New York City. I can see Jesus Christ coming down this great holy highway into a newly furbished Jerusalem with all of His armies of saints and angels, with the populace strung for miles along the highway, to worship and rejoice, and to catch a glimpse of the King of Kings and the Lord of Lords. *"And the ransomed of the Lord shall return, and come to Zion with songs and everlasting joy upon their heads: they shall obtain joy and gladness, and sorrow and sighing shall flee away"* (Isaiah 35:10 KJV).

I cannot overstress the importance of Jesus' reign and new world order being centered in the holy temple as Ezekiel describes. Imagine, if you can, every respective capital of every national government totally dismantled and then replaced with one singular world government with one single world leader—that being King Jesus the Christ. Every law, policy, religious practice, world holiday, and judgment will all be handled directly out of the temple located in the center of a brand new Jerusalem that will be likened unto, as we mentioned, the Garden of Eden. When you see many Christians travelling to Bethlehem each Christmas season to try to relive the birth of Christ, or imagine the annual Mecca pilgrimage of Muslims who travel to Saudi Arabia each year to worship their Allah. Multiply these annual events many times over, then you can begin to imagine the entire surviving world population traveling to Jerusalem each year to the temple where Jesus abides.

If there were ever a world sight to see or visit during the thousand years of Jesus' reign, it will have to be the temple. What other site on earth could compare to the temple in which you could see the Savior of the world in person. This is not a memorial like Mount Rushmore; this is the actual Son of God literally and visually present. You will not see a statute like the Lincoln or Jefferson standing inanimate in their memorials. You will see the King standing regal. If you are a survivor, and you are reading this book, I implore you—go to Jerusalem, go to the temple, and see your Savior immediately.

Chapter Four

The End of Partial Things;
Then the End of Everything

"Love never fails. But where there are prophecies, they will cease; where there are tongues, they will be stilled; where there is knowledge, it will pass away. For we know in part and we prophesy in part, but when perfection comes, the imperfect disappears. Now we see but a poor reflection as in a mirror; then we shall see face to face. Now I know in part; then I shall know fully, even as I am fully known."

(1 Corinthians 13:8-10, 12, NIV).

In this chapter, I would like to show you that there will be an end of things that we have only partial knowledge of in the physical and in the spiritual sense. For instance, we have only partial knowledge of the universe, of ocean floors, or even the sun, moon, stars, our sky, and even the most reachable outer space. All will come to a quick end, as we shall see shortly after the millennial reign is over.

And there will likewise be the end of some spiritual things during the millennial period, such as the gift of tongues and the gift of prophesy, that we use only partially as a Christian to assist the church. You may have noticed that many churches enjoy these gifts of the Holy Spirit, which aid the church in her edification and preservation. Presently, we do not have Him here on the earth to approach, so God has provided His Holy Spirit to subsidize our lack of knowledge through gifts of the Spirit. But even with the gifts of the Spirit, we are still quite limited.

As a spirit-filled Christian, pastoring a spirit-filled church, I have come to rely upon many of the spiritual gifts of the Spirit to direct us in spiritual matters. But even these spiritual gifts are very limited for our use in helping the church members in their faith in God and to live a victorious life in Jesus Christ. The King James Version of 1 Corinthians 13 says that we *"see through a glass darkly,"* or we can barely get a peek, a hint, or a glimpse of some spiritual things such as tongues and their interpretations and prophesy. We are often left with many questions after an interpretation or a prophecy that has been judged legitimate, because we all want to see much further down the road than we are permitted. If we had it our way, we would know everything! But that is not our near future, for the mysteries of God are His to share in His righteous time.

As you might have noticed in the above Scripture (1 Corinthians 13:8-10, 12) Paul singled out to the Corinthians three specific spiritual gifts that will be end upon His arrival at the second coming—knowledge, tongues, and prophecy. I realize that you may not be very knowledgeable or well-read on spiritual gifts, but minimally please know that when Jesus returns, there will be no need for a lot of these spiritual gifts to help us find God. Why? Because God will be on the earth for all to approach without the need for intercessory relationships.

What does it mean, "When perfection comes"?

The Scripture at the beginning of this chapter says, "when that which is perfect shall come." When Jesus returns to rule the kingdom on earth with His scepter of iron, His return will mark the fulfillment of that prophecy. For he is the perfection that will replace all that we knew or thought we knew about everything and anything in this world. Our knowledge here on earth is extremely limited in every literally sense, for we only know things *partially* and not fully or completely. As a survivor, you more than likely believed in Jesus Christ prior to His coming, but for some reason, you did not receive a resurrection or rapture. But He will be the perfection, the completeness, the closure on everything subject under the heavens and above the heavens. Everything you have been looking for in your search to find completeness in your heart of hearts. Jesus will be the perfect judge, governor, leader, and teacher this world will ever know. Whatever has been holding you back from being totally on board with Jesus Christ will be answered in Him. He will be everything you could ever imagine when you see Him with your own eyes.

Partial knowledge will cease

What we know or what we think we know in part (or partially) will vanish because Jesus will come with all knowledge of literally everything we ever wondered about and correct all of the false assumptions we have had about so many things throughout the ages. There has been such great debate, for instance, on the subject of the origin of life and whether or not the universe is the product of a divine design. Similarly, there are ongoing debates as to whether humans were divinely created or the product of evolution, that is, evolving from a much lower species. I also dare to mention the theory that we are the product of insemination from some far off planet or that life arrived here from a crashing asteroid, bringing to earth some kind of stowaway life form that began our species, as we know it today. All these questions will be cleared up when the perfect

One arrives and teaches us all things fully and not partially. But I can assure you that Jesus will show us that all things were created by Him and for Him and by Him do all things consist (Colossians 1:16). I particularly love the way Isaiah says that God will make us to understand that everything was made by Him, *"So that people may see and know, may consider and understand, that the hand of the Lord has done this, that the Holy One of Israel has created it"* (Isaiah 41:20 NIV).

He will clear up all of mankind's scientific opinions, enlighten us on astronomy and the vast universe, on the origins of life and of creation days, of morality, economics, remove our vain philosophies and false beliefs, give explanations of true justice, and the truth about success and beauty–of true riches and prosperity. Things that we know in part like the theories of black holes, of molecules and life existing outside of our own planet, will all be made known in full. We will no longer need to pass on our hypothesis of life to our children or the next generation, for the Lord will teach our children the full truth of all things. *"All your sons will be taught by the Lord, and great will be your children's peace"* (Isaiah 54:13 NIV). The wonders and mysteries of God will not be an agonizing search for truth, for truth will be proclaimed in abundance in His kingdom. The narrow views that we hold onto, and the confused notions we try to propagate will finally whither like petals on a rose.

I find it amusing to read that once the scientific world concludes how many stars and galaxies there are, they stumble upon trillions more. But what is so amazing about the knowledge of God is that He has named each and every star He has created. *"He counts the number of stars and calls them by name"* (Psalm 147:4 NIV). How is that even possible? While God is holding the ever-increasing number of stars in the universe, He knows the numbers of hairs on the heads of every single human on the face of the earth. *"Indeed the very hairs on your head are numbered"*

(Luke 12:7 NIV). How is this possible? There are theories that there are multiple universes, time and space travel wormholes, black holes, the shape of the universe is theoretically flat, life on other planets, the theory of particles, space, sound, and light waves, etc. It's endless what we do not know. But because He is omniscient, He knows everything, He will enlighten us and relieve us of our partial, finite, and erroneous knowledge.

The spiritual gift of knowledge is different than worldly knowledge, but it is still meted out to us partially. The spiritual gift of knowledge is the highest form of knowledge because it is divine by origin. It is a gift to the church in order to bring about an informed church that is founded and rooted in the truth of the gospels.

Also, the Holy Spirit impresses cognitive knowledge that cannot be acquired by information from the world. A person that is gifted in knowledge seems to possess insights and understanding at an exceptional level that is not attainable by just anyone; only to those who are chosen by God. This gift can actually baffle those of the dark world, and can be used to thwart circumstances and strategies of Satan. The gift of knowledge can help churches disarm demons and surprise the unbeliever. But still in all of this, the knowledge remains partial and unclear.

TONGUES WILL CEASE

If you have had experience with the gift of tongues and maybe even the interpretation of tongues, do not expect to find that gift in practice during the thousand-year reign. The supernatural gifts of tongues and the interpretation of tongues will be unnecessary in the millennial. Paul makes it quite clear *"where there are tongues they shall be stilled"* or ceased. Speaking in an unknown tongue is a spiritual gift given to the believer to edify him. It is not a gift that edifies the congregation, because they do not know what the person speaking in tongues is saying without an interpreter. The person speaking in an unknown tongue doesn't understand what he is saying either, for his understanding is unfruitful.

The purpose for speaking in an unknown tongue is to relish in the experience that your spirit is communicating with the Spirit of God, which is self-edifying. Paul says that tongues will cease; meaning the need for speaking or praying in an unknown tongue or the tongues of angels becomes unnecessary when the presence of Jesus Christ is available to you. Tongues will become obsolete because you may approach the throne and speak to the Son of God directly. As a survivor, you are granted the opportunity to speak to Jesus directly, and because of this there is no need for praying in tongues. There will be no need for tongues or an interpreter for us to know what God is trying to say to His people corporately either, because we can hear it directly out of the mouth of Jesus Christ without any confusion or a need for the elders to judge the legitimacy of the interpretation.

When reading different theories as to what language the world will speak on the earth during the thousand-year millennium, I found that some are convinced that we will speak in the pure language in which Adam spoke to God in the Garden of Eden. *"Then I will purify the lips of the peoples, that all of them may call upon the name of the Lord and serve Him shoulder to shoulder"* (Zephaniah 3:9 NIV). Other theorists have offered that we will all speak in the Hebrew language that is native to Jerusalem. Still others theorized that we will all have an undefiled purity of speech, meaning that man will not be given to cussing, swearing, lying, gossiping, using the name of the Lord in vain, backbiting, busy-bodying, bearing false witness, speaking words of death and curses, or words to insult others. I do not know actually what language you will be speaking, but I can assure you, that everyone will be speaking goodness and not wickedness; blessings and not cursing.

Prophecies shall cease

To prophesy is to utter divine inspiration, or even to predict future happenings or events as inspired by the Holy Spirit. Prophecies will be superseded by the words of Jesus Christ, and thank God for clarity in the Spirit. Paul instructs the Corinthians that two or three men will judge as to the authenticity of all prophecies. There will be no need for men to judge the words of Jesus Christ as to His correctness or accuracy, for who can judge the Lord Jesus? I will suggest that Jesus will prophesy largely concerning the events that will take place after the thousand-year reign ends with the release of Satan, and the attack of Gog and Magog (Russia). Jesus will also interpret all the prophesies of Him mentioned in the Old Testament—from the Torah through the major and minor prophets. There are New Testament Scriptures in the Book of Revelation that contain prophecies that are yet to be fulfilled at this point, and I am sure that Jesus will address those prophecies as well.

The absolute finality of everything

If you manage to survive the full millennium from the beginning, this would make you well over one thousand years old. You are doing quite well at this point; however, there is one last challenge that will come to the earth that you must overcome to be successful. You have noticed that the world (during the millennial period) is a near-perfect world without sickness, economic hardships, poverty, hunger, or political manipulation by men that would try to become a greater leader than Jesus Christ.

But all of that will come to a sudden end at the near close of the thousand years, and you will be hurled into a storm of contention. You will witness the buildup of an army, and even the releasing of Satan who will attempt to overthrow God one more time.

The earth has been free of this most-evil spirit called Satan for one thousand years, with Jesus Christ leading the world in true tranquility and safety from marauders or despot leaders looking to hurt and kill others. The vast majority of the population has been birthed during the millennial, so they would have only heard stories of Satan, fallen angels, demons, spiritual warfare, and physical wars, for that matter. They may only have seen memorials or remnants of the last world war and Armageddon. This population didn't experience what we presently fight against; that is, unseen dark spirits that tempt or cause us to fall into sin and then die. When God allows the archangel to release Satan for one more season, there will be immediate chaos, temptations, confusions, and offensiveness, everywhere. Many hearts will falter from God if they are not careful. There will be a quick organizing of a mighty army, very massive in numbers, that will be opposed to everything Jesus represents. Be sure to stay away from these dissenters, because they will come to a quick end by the hand of God.

"And when the thousand years are expired, Satan shall be loosed out of his prison. And shall go out to deceive the nations which are in the four quarters of the earth, Gog and Magog, to gather them together to battle: the number of whom is as the sand of the sea. And they went up on the breadth of the earth, and compassed the camp of the saints, and the beloved city: and fire came down out of heaven, and devoured them." (Revelation 20:7-9 KJV)

Mankind has been prepared for this war through the teachings and prophesies of King Jesus and of the priests of the earth who are privy to the Scriptures. These teachings, along with the teachings of the Torah, will have been taught since the beginning of the millennium, so this war will not come as a surprise. However, it's one thing to learn about Satan's wily darts, but a completely different matter to experience the actual sensation of being tempted by him. But please remember, Satan has always been a tool that God uses to test the faithfulness of His people and all of His angels. Satan is not an all-powerful, all-seeing god; he is actually quite limited and has nowhere near the ability of any of God's powerful angels, let alone God Almighty. Satan is not the opposite of God, because he is a creation of God. Satan is but a mere fallen angel whom God will destroy once his use has expired. Actually, when the saints see Satan for the first time, they will be surprised at his weakness and vulnerability. Isaiah really helps us put Satan's vulnerability into perspective. *"Those who see you will gaze at you (Satan), they will ponder over you saying, Is this the man who made the earth to tremble, who shook kingdoms, who made the world like a wilderness and overthrew cities"* (Isaiah 14:16-17 NASB). This war will be the last the war that angels and mankind will ever experience. The opposition will be solely concentrated on one rogue nation, Gog and Magog (or Russia). Satan will lure the Russian government to build up a great army in order to attack Israel, specifically Jerusalem, that will be the headquarters of King Jesus (Revelation 20:1-3, 7-9).

I find this final war an enigma, because after an extended lifetime of world peace without even a hint of a skirmish, why would the world be sucked back into another war? I realize it is because man's heart will wane and the reentry of Satan is a substantial influence, but the Scriptures say that those who will oppose Jesus will be so massive, that it can be compared to the number of sand in the sea! I suppose I am perplexed at the vast number of those who fall away, much like those who were destroyed in the Great Flood of Noah's day, and just like those who perished in sin one thousand years prior during the second coming of Christ. Once again, and please forgive me for the repetition, but do not associate with these rebellious people who want to overthrow Jesus and kill His people.

I believe that this war will act as the last move of God, to extract those who would choose to oppose Him, Jesus Christ's government, and of course, the nation of Israel. If you find yourself among these dissenters – then I regret to say that your time has come to an end. However, it is my hope that, if you find yourself vacillating on a decision, you will choose correctly. Choose Jesus Christ and do not be tempted by Satan or any political propaganda. Just remember, in all of the confusion, the nation that takes a stand against Israel is the side you do not want to be on. It will be as simple as that. No matter what the press or the voice of the opposition says about what the Jews are doing or not doing – just keep it simple and choose Jesus, Jerusalem, and Israel.

YOUR PERSONAL CHOICES
AND YOUR FREE WILL

As I mentioned in the introduction, it is not in my belief that a man has no ability to choose. This idea is the foundation of Calvinism, which I feel, is damaging to true Christianity. True Christianity is all about making a personal choice, against all odds, for Jesus to be your Lord and Savior. I believe that God gave us the ability to choose blessings or cursing, life or death, and holiness over unrighteousness and wickedness. Since you as a survivor have been given so many opportunities to choose correctly for Jesus Christ (who, incidentally, is the only pathway to the Father and Heaven), I am optimistic that you will continue to choose Him through this last vetting of God and the angels. If, per chance, you were either forced to participate in this rebellion or die, it would be good for you to choose death rather than stand off against holiness and righteousness. Your martyrdom will certainly translate into enormous rewards and recompense once you arrive in heaven.

God Almighty, at this point, will allow man to arm himself and begin to construct a plot to destroy Jesus' government. I expect Satan's Gog and Magog will include cleverly hidden snares, pitfalls, or traps that will try to tempt you in ceasing your long journey with Jesus Christ. I especially suspect that Russia will have refused and/or prevented its inhabitants to make the mandatory annual pilgrimage to Jerusalem, and because of these acts of defiance, they have had droughts and the resultant famines, which in turn can bring on anger against God. This national anger can manifest into a unified rebellion to overthrown the world government of Jesus. Satan will take this opportunity to reteach man (Russia, in this case) how to make weapons of war and to train men to kill once again.

I do not know if Russia will devise a plan to create alliances with other nations that are equally rebellious; the Scriptures are not clear on this. The Scripture is quite clear, however, that the number of militants will be commensurate with the sands of the sea, and capable of encompassing all of the children of God, the saints, and all of Jerusalem and Israel. We mentioned a few times that though the population of the earth after the second coming will be extremely small, procreation during the millennial period will be unprecedented. There will be many children being born from mothers who will not experience birth pains, and there will not be any abortions, nor birth defects or Sudden Infant Death Syndrome (SIDS), or economical influences to deter having many children. So, there will be many people upon the face of the earth. But I will say very freely that this war will not be a long war. And no matter how many people oppose Christ in this massive world population, God will send fire from heaven to destroy (actually it says "devour") this opposition very quickly and deliberately.

Why does Jesus relinquish the Kingdom to the Father?

The primary mandate during the thousand years of King Jesus is to destroy all evil, sin, all rebellion, and all those who oppose His government and Israel, and to put all things under His feet–in other words, to put everything and everyone in total subjection to Him. This is the reason why His reign is equipped with an iron scepter; once Jesus has destroyed all evil, and this includes the destruction of the last opposing armies of Russia, He will turn a purged and vetted Kingdom over to the Almighty Father for Him to reign over everything.

*"Then cometh the end, when He shall have delivered up the Kingdom to God, even the Father; when He shall have put down all rule and all authority and power. For He must reign, till He hath put all enemies under His feet. The last enemy that shall be destroyed is death. For He hath put all things under His feet. But when He saith all things are put under Him, it is manifest that He is excepted, which did put all things under Him. And when all things shall be subdued unto Him, **then shall the Son also Himself be subject unto Him that put all things under Him, that God maybe all in all"** *(1 Corinthians 15:24-28 KJV).

Actually, Jesus uses the one thousand years of His reign to remove all authority from any man or spirit, and to present the Kingdom as a tribute to God Almighty. But the Kingdom cannot have any rogue leader, any lone despot, any evil cell groups that are plotting, or any criminal minds that would oppose the Kingdom authority. His intentions are to destroy the existence of Satan, the false prophet, the Antichrist, all the nations and armies that oppose Israel, all rebellious angels of heaven, all the fallen angels, demons and every evil spirit that roams the earth and air, and even all creatures that are possessed with evil spirits. Because of Jesus Christ, there can only be a zero-tolerance-for-sin government under His reign. For at the end of the millennial period, all of His enemies must be vanquished, His ordinances and Law must be adhered to, and all wicked and ungodly men must be subjected to His wrath.

"Thou hast put all in in subjection under His feet. For in that He put all in subjection under Him, He left nothing that is not put under Him. But now we see not yet all things put under Him" (Hebrews 2:8 KJV).

Amazingly enough, King David prophesied in Psalms 110:1 (KJV) that the Kingdom would be put under Jesus Christ as well, *"The Lord said unto my Lord, sit thou at my right hand, until I make thine enemies thy footstool."* Since the time Jesus walked the earth as a man, He has represented God to us in so many ways. He mediates for us to the Father so as to procure mercy: *"For there is one God and one mediator between God and mankind, the man Christ Jesus"* (1 Timothy 2:5 KJV). Even now Jesus is interceding for us at the right hand of God (Romans 8:34). Jesus taught us how to pray to God, how to perceive the character of God, and about the Old Testament prophecies of the eventual end of all things. But there is coming a day when there will be no need for an intercessor or judge, for all wickedness and sin will be completely gone forever. Though Jesus Christ will become the light of the New City, (Revelation 21:23), He will return to a status that will reunite Him back into a oneness with the Almighty God (John 17:21-22).

The Final Burning and Vanquishing of the Entire Earth and Sky

"But the day of the Lord will come as a thief in the night; in the which the heavens shall pass away with a great noise, and the elements shall melt with fervent heat, the earth also and the works therein shall be burned up. Seeing then that all these things shall be dissolved, what manner of persons ought ye to be in all holy conversation and godliness? Looking to and hasting unto the coming of the day of God, wherein the heavens being on fire shall dissolved, and the elements shall melt with fervent heat? Nevertheless we, according to His promise, look for new

heavens and a new earth, wherein dwelleth righteousness" (2 Peter 10-13 KJV).

If you are a survivor at this point, you would have already been judged and residing in heaven or in the lake of fire for all eternity. You are no longer a mortal either way, because mortality no longer exists. As a survivor, you have been judged based upon how you lived your long life on the earth during the thousand years. You were most certainly judged on your faithfulness to Jesus Christ and whether you rebelled or opposed Him as the King of Kings. You would have been judged based upon whether or not you were deceived by the return of Satan and if you participated as an opposition against His kingdom during the Magog war. Either way, this is truly the end of everything mortal and terrestrial.

The first worldwide destruction was the great flood in which Noah and his family (a total of eight souls) were the only human survivors. The second worldwide destruction will be the terrible day of the Lord in which a small population of the world will survive; we discussed this already in prior chapters. Conversely, the destruction of all things is vastly different in that everything, and everyone, including the earth, will be destroyed, and there will be no life of any kind. Planet Earth will be vanquished. God will accomplish this destruction with a very extreme fire. It will be an incomprehensible fire that is coupled with a very loud noise that seems to emphasize immediate and abrupt destruction. Fire has always represented a purifying process.

THE END OF THE HUMAN SPECIES

What we know of the human body began with the creation of Adam in which God created him literally from the soil of the earth and breath from His spiritual lungs. Man began to procreate from that point and has continued each and every day since.

With a current average life expectancy of sixty-seven, UNICEF estimates an average of 353,000 births per day. From the creation of Adam until now, there is estimated to have been seven billion humans alive on the planet earth. According to Deevey (1960) he has estimated all humans who have been born to a total of 110 billion. The Guinness Book of Records (1983) estimated that 75,000,000,000 people have born and died throughout human history. According to *Aid to Understanding*, (1971, page 1400); and *Insight on the Scriptures* (1988 Volume 2, p. 792), both liberally cite that only twenty billion humans have been born and died since the creation of Adam. Though it seems to be a matter of how many years the researcher has estimated how long mankind has been on the earth. But no matter who is correct in their estimations, in the face of these incredible populations, there will be an end of human births and deaths at the final vanquishing of the earth and heavens, for it will be the end of the human era forever.

The end of all elements

Peter described the true end of literally everything—and this is the end. The end of the entire world and earth as we know it. It is the end of human beings as mortals, the end of the earth and our atmosphere as we know it. There will be virtually nothing left that is recognizable to our mortal eyes. God Almighty will create a brand new earth and a new heaven, and there will be no moon, or a sun, or seas. I would suspect that our entire solar system would no longer exist, for without the gravitational pull of the sun, the nine planets would be free to roam the universe– free-floating, as it were. Imagine a new earth that is not revolving around a sun and without rotation that determines night and day.

This description by the apostle Peter leaves nothing left of the old earth. When we read Peter mentioning the melting of all *elements,* I am reminded of my geography and physics lessons. There are four elements in our earth: water, air, earth, and fire, and certainly creatures and humans are made up of a few of these elements.

Vanishing of all water

When Peter is speaking of all forms of water being eradicated, he is speaking of oceans, seas, rivers, streams, lakes, ponds, creeks, vapor, condensation, fog and clouds, all organics that contain water, as well as the waters below. All will be totally evaporated away. This would also include every living creature and human being. From the whale to the ant, from the elephant to the microbe—all life forms that require water to survive will be destroyed.

Vanishing of all air

When Peter speaks of the melting of the air as an element, he is referring to our colorful skies and clouds, which includes our nitrogen, oxygen, carbon dioxide, argon, water vapor, and moisture.

Vanishing of all the earth

When Peter speaks of the element of the earth, he prophesies that all the earth is melted away– from the earth's crust to its mantel– all of the earth's soil and rock will be dissolved. John the revelator also writes very clearly that there will be no moon or a sun (Revelation 21:23). For that matter, after the end of all things there will not even be a night sky or an evening (Revelation 21:25). Although after the second coming of Jesus Christ and during His great millennium, there will be a need for the sun and moon as previously mentioned, but after this virtual end comes, there will be no need. After the end comes, there will be no tears, no crying, no death, no sorrow or pain, (Revelation 21:4). During the millennial, there will be found those who will rebel against the reign of Jesus Christ, but there will not be a single person that will sin after the very end of all things (Revelation 2:8, 27).

Every single sinner will have been destroyed. Every single evil spirit, or demon, will have been damned to the Lake of Fire. There are actually three spiritual enemies of a man: his flesh, the world, and Satan. And all of these three spiritual enemies will, at this point, be destroyed. All of God's people will be immortal and all the unbelievers and the wicked will be thrown into eternal judgment, and Satan will have been thrown into the Lake of Fire as well. There will be no more evil when the end has come. Please make no mistake between the destruction that occurs at the second coming of Jesus Christ and the final destruction at the end of all things. This can be seen very clearly when we recognize that many of the elements, sin and rebellion, the sun and moon and evenings, crying and death, still very much exist during the thousand years of Jesus' government.

Also, please realize that during the thousand years of Jesus Christ, Jesus repairs the earth, He doesn't, as yet, make a new earth. He takes the destroyed earth and rebuilds it, especially Israel where He repairs it like the Garden of Eden. After the end of all things, there will be a new earth, not a repaired one. *"He who is seated on the throne said, I am making everything new...!"* (Revelation 21:5 NIV). There's a big difference between a repaired car and a brand new car. It's not remodeled or redesigned, but new. And the new earth is certainly not put together with existing materials. We do not know what the new earth will look like but it will certainly be different that this existing one. *"For, behold, I create **new heavens and a new earth: and the former shall not be remembered, nor come to mind**"* (Isaiah 65:17 KJV). Notice that no one will recall, or care to recall, former things of old. We will live as immortals, among immortals, and not have a mind for our former life or even remember them. Our humanity will be finally put to rest and we shall only be pressing forward. Many have asked will we remember our lives on earth once we are raptured, and I believe the answer is tentatively yes. Yes, in so much as during the thousand years we will recall our former life in order to help others gain a victory. And also, we are rewarded for those things which we have accomplished on earth, so they must be remembered. However, I do not believe that after we have seen the final end of the earth, we will remember anything. There will be no need to recall those days, for heaven is a place filled only with the inexhaustible presence of the love of God Almighty.

TRUE HEAVEN IS THE CITY OF
NEW JERUSALEM

What actual heaven will be like is literally unimaginable. *"No eye has seen no ear has heard, no mind has conceived what God has prepared for those who love Him"* (1 Corinthians 2:9 NIV). And this is where I pray and hope you are striving to be. Your mistake would be to aim too low—to be only a survivor on the earth. It will be very difficult, as you have seen, to survive. However, if you want to become a resurrected saint, reach for Jesus now before it's too late.

There is a difference between paradise and heaven (the city of New Jerusalem). Paradise you can read about in the book of Luke chapter 16. There you will meet a rich man who dies and goes to hell and a poor man named Lazarus who dies and goes to a place called Abraham's bosom – or paradise. Paradise is the waiting place for all those who died and are awaiting the rapture (for we will all enter into heaven together on the day of the rapture, both those who are dead and alive in Christ. Though heaven is wondrous and beautiful – there is no comparing it to the city of New Jerusalem, which is true heaven. This is the place in which Paul is telling the Corinthians that eye hath not seen, ear not heard, nor mind conceived what God has prepared for those who love Him. I have read and also watched on You Tube many testimonies of out-of-body experiences and near death experiences. Most have testified seeing a Paradise that is absolutely beautiful. But I do not believe that anyone has seen what God has beyond those walls that surround the New City – the residency of God, Jesus Christ, and the people of God. We are all in for a huge surprise that is going to be a resident in this walled community. I do hope that this is your aspiration! Heaven is a fascinating place to ponder, especially when we see millions of readers pour over New York Times best-selling books in which authors, as mentioned, testify as to their out-of-body experiences (OBE) or their near-death experiences (NDE) and their respective journey to heaven. Books such as *90 Minutes in Heaven, Heaven is for Real,* or *To Heaven and Back* have intrigued believers and unbelievers alike.

  The new earth and the new heavens (Revelation 21:1-2), and of course the New City of Jerusalem will be created beyond our wildest dreams– this is truly Heaven. It is impossible for a human being to imagine what God has been preparing for us that love Him. Hollywood does some amazing things with their special effects, but they cannot begin to fathom the beauty and glory of what God is building for us. You will notice that in Revelation 21 there is a detailed description of the Heavenly City of New Jerusalem that boasts of being 1500 square miles of majestic crystal. The very idea that this city reaches 1500 miles straight up from the new earth and into space (space begins at the height of sixty miles from the surface of the earth) is physically impossible without its builder and maker being God Almighty. This would mean that the city would be stretching into outer space some 1400-plus miles. For me personally, I find this incomprehensible, yet exhilarating.

Imagine a building that reaches 1500 miles in terms of elevators, floors, or stories. If each story were measured to be ten feet, then a 1500-mile building would require 792,000 stories. If each story were given a twenty-foot clearance, then there would be 396,000 floors or stories. That's incredible when you consider that the Empire State Building is only one hundred and two stories and requires two elevators to get to the top. Imagine an elevator for a building with 792,000 floors. Obviously heavenly citizens will not require elevators, for I am sure that immortals travel at the speed of thought. If you were to stand upon the earth, you could not physically see the top of a building that stands fifteen hundred miles into space.

To reach 1500 miles from the earth's surface would mean passing through the troposphere, which is the lowest layer of earth's atmosphere and the location of all weather on earth, taking up 60,000 feet in depth of our sky. The tallest building in the world barely reaches three thousand feet high. So this alone is twenty times higher than any building in the world (and lest we forget, the city is also 1500 miles wide as well). The height of the city would pass through the stratosphere, which is 160,000 feet or thirty miles toward near space. The city continues to stretch into the mesosphere, which peaks at 285,000 feet or fifty-four miles high. The city passes through the next layer of space known as the thermosphere, which reaches 400,000 feet into space (seventy-five miles). The city eventually reaches half-way to the exosphere, some six thousand miles into deeper space. This God-made building/city will probably sit right upon where the old city of Jerusalem sat, and will be the crown jewel of the New Earth for all the people of God.

WHY ARE THE HEAVENS GOING TO BE DESTROYED?

In considering all of the above, there are a few reasons why the Lord will destroy the heavens (Revelation 21:1-2): First, there are enormous amounts of man-made debris floating in Earth's orbit. Specifically, there are 2,600 non-functioning satellites, 1,100 functioning satellites, and an innumerable amount of scattered tools, fragments of collided satellites, and other various space junk–all orbiting the earth right now. As a matter of fact, there is a projection that there will be such an increase of accumulated space debris by the year 2020 that it will be near impossible for future space flights to enter space without crashing into floating junk. I don't see the Lord tolerating the existence of the space debris – I imagine He will destroy it all with a fervent heat as He will the earth.

A CLOSER LOOK AT THE THRONE OF GOD THROUGH THE EYES OF ENOCH

I make mention in the introduction of the splendid descriptions of the throne of God through the eyes of Enoch, which pushed my imagination and brightened up my excitement to see His mightiness and glory. And as I continue to read these passages and many just like them, I am caught between a euphoric awe and a tremendous fear of His terrible greatness. Please note in the selections below the awesome power that is frightfully and vividly present at the throne of God and the many angels that stand around the throne. I do not hesitate or balk at estimating their numbers in the trillions. And of course, note the raptured people, which I hope you are viewing with the aspiration to be one. Look at this majestic display of God told by Enoch:

"And I went in till I drew nigh to a wall which is built of crystals and surrounded by tongues of fire: and it began to affright me. A flaming fire surrounded the walls, and its portals blazed with fire. And its floor was on fire, and above it were lightnings and the path of stars, and its ceiling also was flaming fire. And I looked and saw therein a lofty throne: its appearance was crystal, and the wheels thereof as the shining sun, and there was the vision of cherubim. And from underneath the throne

came streams of flaming fire so that I could not look thereon. And the Great Glory sat thereon, and His raiment shone more brightly than the sun and was whiter than any snow. None of the angels could enter and could behold His face by reason of the magnificence and glory, and no flesh could behold Him. The flaming fire was all about Him, and a great fire was before Him, and none around Him could draw nigh Him: ten thousand times ten thousands stood before Him, yet He needed no counselor. (Enoch 14:9, 12, 17-22)

"And it came to pass after this that my spirit was translated and it ascended into the heavens: And I saw the holy sons of God. They were stepping on flames of fire: Their garments were white and their raiment, and their faces shone like snow. And I saw two streams of fire, and the light of that fire shone like hyacinth, and I fell on my face before the Lord of Spirits. And the angel Michael, one of the archangels, seized me by my right hand, and lifted me up and led me forth into all secrets, and he showed me all the secrets of righteousness. And he showed me all the secrets of the ends of the heaven, and all the chambers of the stars, and all the luminaries, whence they proceed before the face of the holy ones. And he translated my spirit into the heaven of heavens, and I saw there as it were a structure built of crystals, and between those crystals tongues of living fire. And my spirit saw the girdle, which girt that house of fire, and on its four sides were streams full of living fire, and they girt that house. And round about were Seraphim, Cherubim, and Ophannin: and these are they who slept not and guard the throne of His glory. And I saw angels who could not be counted, a thousand thousands, and ten thousand times ten thousand, encircling that house, and Michael and Raphael, and Gabriel, and Phanuel, and the holy angels who are above the heavens, go in and out of that house. And they came forth from that house, and Michael and Gabriel, Raphael and Phanuel, and many holy angels without number. And with them the Head of Days, His head white and pure as wool, and His raiment was indescribable. And I fell on my face, and my whole body became relaxed, and my spirit was transfigured; and I cried with a loud voice,

and with the spirit of power, and blessed and glorified and extolled. And these blessings, which went forth out of my mouth, were well pleasing before that Head of Days. And that Head of Days came with Michael and Gabriel, Raphael and Phanuel, thousands and ten thousands of angels without number. And he (the angel) came to me and greeted me with His voice, and said unto me: This is the Son of Man who is born unto righteousness, and righteousness abides over Him; and the righteousness of the Head of Days forsakes Him not." (Enoch 71:1-14)

As you can clearly see, Enoch further exalts the power of God, and does not add anything that is outside the doctrine of our accepted canon, the Book of Revelation, or within our sense of correctness. The fire we see in and around the throne and the Lord God Almighty represents not just the power of God, but also the purifying that leaves only the most valuable and tried-by-fire matter.

This is why the entire earth will be totally destroyed by fire, because there will be nothing on it or in it that is worth saving. The earth will have seen so much sin, absorbed so much bloodshed, and experienced the enormity of wickedness, that nothing good will remain. Fire purifies and starts things fresh and new. There is nothing that God plans to retain on earth or in the world. God will destroy all sources of sinful pollutants and nothing that is evil or wicked can approach the throne of God, for it is engulfed in innumerable tons of cleansing and frightening fire. The very foundation of God is not love as many would surmise, but rather it is holiness. And fire, divine fire, will purge everything and everyone – and nothing that is not purged or baptized by fire can approach the throne of God.

Please find below, three scriptures from the book of Enoch that share with the reader the engulfing fire that is found in heaven, among the angels, and the face and throne of God Almighty. You will see that Enoch only enhances Scriptures of the Bible that speak about the divine, purifying fires of heaven that you will witness if you have had a good journey after your initial survival. Though I have underlined the phrases that speak of purifying fire, please try to grasp each entire passage. They are full of fantastic descriptions of heaven:

1.) *"And I saw there an exceptionally great light, and **all the fiery armies of the great archangels,** and the incorporeal forces and the dominions and the origins and the authorities, the cherubim and the seraphim and the many-eyed thrones; and regiments and the shining otanim stations. **And I was terrified, and I trembled with a great fear.** And those [angels] picked me up and led me into their midst. And they said unto me, 'Be brave, Enoch! Don't be frightened.' And they showed me the Lord, from a distance, sitting on his exceedingly high throne. ... And all the heavenly armies came and stood on the ten steps, corresponding to their ranks, and they did obeisance to the Lord. And then they went to places in joy and merriment and in immeasurable light, singing songs with soft and gentle voices, while presenting liturgy to Him gloriously."* (Enoch 20:1-4)

2.) *"I saw the view of **the face of the Lord, like iron made burning hot in a fire** and brought out, and it emits sparks and is incandescent. Thus even I saw the face of the Lord. But the face of the Lord is not to be talked about, it is so very marvelous and supremely awesome and supremely frightening. And who am I to give an account of the incomprehensible being of the Lord, and of His face, so extremely strange and indescribable? And how many are His commands, and His multiple voices, and the Lord's throne, cherubim and the seraphim armies, and their never silent singing. Who can give an account of His beautiful appearance, never changing and indescribable, and His great glory? And I fell down flat and did obeisance to the Lord. And the Lord, with His own mouth, said to me, 'be brave, Enoch! Don't be frightened! Stand up, and stand in front of My face forever. And Michael, the Lord's greatest angel, lifted me up and brought me in front* *of the face of the Lord. And the Lord sounded out His servants. The Lord said, 'Let Enoch come up and stand in front of my face forever!' And the glorious ones did obeisance and said, let him come up! The Lord said to Michael, 'Take up Enoch, and extract him from the earthly clothing. And anoint him with delightful oil, and put him into clothes of glory. And Michael extracted me from my clothes. He anointed me with delightful oil; and the appearance of that oil is great than the greatest light, its ointment is like sweet dew, and its fragrance like myrrh; and its shining is like the sun. And I gazed at myself, and I had become like one of the glorious ones, and there was no observable difference."* (Enoch 22:1-10)

3.) ***"For the lips of the Lord are a furnace of fire, and His angels are flames which come out.*** *But I am one who has seen the face of the Lord,* ***like iron made burning hot by a fire, and it is brought out and it omits sparks and it is incandescent.*** *But you gaze into my eyes, a human being equal in significance to yourselves; but I have gazed into the eyes of the* ***Lord, shining like the rays of the sun and terrifying*** *...."* (Enoch 39:5b)

THE WHITE THRONE JUDGMENT FOR
EVERY HUMAN WHO DOESN'T RECEIVE A RESURRECTION

The White Throne Judgment is the final judgment God Almighty will preside over according to every scripture we have available to us. It seems that everyone who appears before this judgment is not, more than likely, going to fair well. But I cannot know this conclusively. This judgment, which takes place before the terrifying throne of the Almighty God, will judge all of the dead that never received a rapture or a resurrection—either during the *main event* rapture, during the tribulation where many will be raptured as martyrs, or those who died and rose during the millennium. The rest of the dead will not rise until the last judgment. This is why I theorize that it will not fare well for those who stand before this judgment throne. You will note that *"death and hell"* are both cast into the lake of fire. I presume, as many have, that these are those who are in a hell that has only one next stop – the lake of fire.

"Then I saw a great white throne and Him who was seated on it. The earth and the heavens fled from His presence, and there was no place for them. And I saw the dead, the great and the small, standing before the throne, and books were opened; and another book was opened, which is the book of life; and the dead were judged from these, which were written in the books, according to their deeds. And the sea gave up the dead, who were in it, and death and hell gave up the dead, who were in them; and they were judged, every one of them according to their deeds. Then death and hell were thrown into the lake of fire. This is the second death, the lake of fire. And if anyone's name was not found written in the book of life, he was thrown in the lake of fire." (Revelation 20:13-15 NIV)

We can only pray that the white throne judgment will offer much mercy and grace to those who stand before Him. These that stand before the white throne judgment are those who have been dead since the death of Cain to the present day; there will be an unfathomable number of people who will be called for judgment.

THERE IS NO ANNIHILATION OF
THE WICKED AND EVIL PEOPLE

Annihilation in the Latin root is *nihil* or nothing. The meaning from this root is to literally make into nothing. Annihilation is to make a complete obliteration of a person or object. It describes the total destruction and nonexistence of something or someone. When a person is under the belief that once they die and go to hell they will merely burn up and no longer exist, they surmise that there will be an initial pain of burning to death, but then the bliss of nonexistence will finally relieve their pain and suffering. However, this belief has no valid foundation. The Scriptures say that the fire is forever and the suffering is constant day and night. *"And the smoke of their torment goes up forever and ever; they have no rest day and night"* (Revelation 14:11 NIV).

The regretful thing about mankind going to the eternal lake of fire is that the fire was never intended or created for man but, rather, for Satan and his fallen angels. *"Then shall he say also unto the left hand, depart from Me, ye accursed, into **everlasting fire, prepared for the devil and his angels"** (Matthew 25:41 KJV). Many are convinced that certain men and women are predestined to go to hell or heaven directly from birth (or sooner), and that there is nothing that the person can do to change such a predetermined destiny. However, God never intended for anyone to go to hell. The Bible says it is not His will that any should perish, but for everyone to come to Him and repent of their sins and misdeeds. And since hell was never created initially for fallen man, then actually all of man was predestined to be with Him in heaven. Sadly, it's you and I that complicate this destiny of ours, not God.

Imagine, if you would, no hope forever and forever for an exit from damnation. It is not a sentence of years to suffer penitence and then to escape tormenting fire and be welcomed into heaven for eternity. The judgment of eternal damnation is once and for all with no hope for mercy or grace. Imagine also, and this is terrifying in itself, being eternally alienated from God; to never hear His voice, feel His presence, experience His kindness, or to see His love working for you. It is also terrifying to not only be alienated from God, but to never fellowship with the saints of the living God. Many may not presently relish the company of the righteous until they are separated from them. And needless to say, there will be no righteous in the tormenting fires of

137

damnation. This would mean that there will be no one to ask for help and prayer, or intercession, or even acts of kindness. To exist throughout eternity in the absence of goodness is an unimaginable loss.

THE CLOSING OF THE DOORS

I fully realize that writing, speaking, or even alluding to hell and the lake of fire is a difficult thing to read about. I have been a pastor for going on forty years, and I have come to realize that if you want a steadily growing church, you stay off of the taboo subjects of punishment, consequences, sins of the flesh and spirit, hell, and the lake of fire. Obviously, these words and phrases are not conducive to a church-growth program. These words are offensive to most and more than likely open to great debate as to the truth or existence of them. I know that if I would steer clear of challenging a congregation with these frightful and judgmental words, it would mean a faster growing church that would possibly result in much more money in the church coffers. The church I pastor, on any given good-attendance week, is between 1,800 to 2,000 members, but I know that if we were to adopt a more hyper-grace focus, by not even suggesting that some adherents may end up in hell, our church could be running twice as much. But I, like many other ministers of the Gospel, know that if we remain quiet in order to gain more members or more giving, then we would be like a dog that cannot bark, like a watchman that cannot warn, like a minister that withholds the truth.

If you are presently reading this book during this wonderful time of grace, mercy, and the quick and open forgiveness of Jesus Christ, please know that you can escape all of the coming judgment and be swept away into a most beautiful place where there is righteousness and goodness everywhere. Today you can be forgiven, but tomorrow is not promised to any of us. Today is the day of salvation, now is the accepted hour (2 Corinthians 6:2).

One can clearly read that the divine benefits of heaven outweigh any treasures here on the earth. And the wisdom of the Father, if you will have Him, is far more insightful than that of any man you will discover. Though one would find Christianity a difficult life to live, I would say to you that the resulting end is very much worth your time, treasure, and trouble. This is actually a time when Jesus stands knocking at your door to be let into your life. But as you read in this modest work, one day all doors will be closed to those who did not want Him to come into their lives. That will most certainly be a torturous life indeed. Save yourself then, my friend, from this untoward world, and bask in the glory of the One who has come to retrieve you. It's a closing choice of yours, and no one else's.

Won't you come and follow us, as we in turn, follow Christ?

APPENDIX A

Books of Enoch and 2 Baruch

I freely use the extra-biblical books of Enoch and 2 Baruch interchangeably as supporting material for the following reasons:

1. The church fathers knew and used these two books and called them Holy Scripture. These church fathers: Justin Martyr, Irenaeus, Origen, Clement, and Tertullian, all have agreed with other canonizations—specifically the Ethiopic Canon (established as early as 50-100 AD), the Essene Canon, and the Apocrypha. James H. Charlesworth, director of Dead Sea scrolls at Yale University stated, "I have no doubt that the Enoch groups deemed the Book of Enoch fully inspired as any biblical book." Charlesworth also believed that the Jews behind the Temple Scroll also judged the BOE to be quintessential Torah, or equal to, and perhaps better than, Deuteronomy. *Liberty Magazine* back in December 7, 1935, wrote, "For more than a century, scholars and church officials debated as to whether or not certain gospels, epistles, and apocalypses should be included. For instance, it was long debated which to included in the canon, the Book of Revelation or the Book of Enoch..."

2. Jude quoted Enoch in the Bible, and fragments of Enoch were found among the Dead Sea scrolls. Some researchers believe that most major themes of the New Testament were in fact "borrowed" from the BOE. The term "watchers" is patently from the BOE. Daniel uses the term to refer to fallen angels (Daniel 4:13, 17, 23 KJV). Also see Strong's 5894 defining "watchers" as angels.

3. The BOE actually gave the Jews their solar calendar, and the belief that the Messiah would be someone that preexisted with God.

4. Because the Book of Enoch prophesies about Jesus Christ (Enoch 46:1-2; 47:5,7; 48:2-7), *the Jews refused to canonize the book. And because Martin Luther demanded that the Christians should only canonize the books the Jews canonize, they in turn refused the Book of Enoch during the Council of Laodicea.* The Laodicea Council also attempted to remove the Book of Revelation, but the Council of Carthage superseded their attempts. However, in spite of the Laodicean's desire to exclude the Book of Enoch, the Council of Nicene plagiarized their theology directly from the BOE. The book slowly went out of print and disappeared until it was rediscovered in the 1770s. But for the first three centuries after Jesus ascended, the Book of Enoch was equally as accepted as the other sixty-six books.

5. One must recognize that the Book of Enoch was not merely rejected for canonization, but was suppressed, intentionally lost, buried, and banned, with all copies destroyed or left to rot ten stories deep under the Vatican. Origen, a church father, stated that this (disappearance of the Book of Enoch) was the most successful, enduring, and damaging cover-up of the truth.

Another church father, Tertullian, stated that the Jews corrupted their own scriptures to remove Jesus from the Old Testament. So because a reader can see the prophesy of Jesus Christ in the Book of Enoch, the Jews then rejected the BOE, because it in fact teaches the Messiah as Jesus. "Since Enoch, in the same scripture, also taught about the Lord, then it should be not rejected by us … But it appears that the Jews rejected it specifically for that reason,

just like they do almost every other part that foretells Christ."
(Tertullian, *"On the Apparel of Woman"*, 1:3) One of the biggest
problems the Jews have with the BOE is the use of the term "Son
of Man" as the Messianic title. This is what Jesus was referring
to in the Gospels when He said He was the Son of Man; He was
referring to Himself as the Messiah, as cited in the BOE. The
Jewish community all too well knew this in His day. They knew
exactly what He was saying. And this is the reason they wanted
to stone Him for blasphemy, because the term "Son of Man" is
conducive with the Messiah.

1. One last point regarding the BOE is that it helped me with
    explaining the wrongly theorized extraterrestrials visiting
    the earth, planetary travelers, alien abductions, UFOs,
    space spirit guides, cults, and even interbreeding of space
    visitors and humans. My intent is not to take a wide brush
    and minimize people's experiences of what they believed to
    be extraterrestrials. I will offer, however, a more palatable
    explanation to these intense testimonies of sighting and
    abductions. The BOE discusses very candidly fallen
    angels that are among us that have influenced mankind
    for millennia through advanced technology in order to
    turn mankind to sinful practices. For me, it is a far better
    consideration than believing intellectual beings from distant
    planets have inseminated humans and live among us. The
    Book of Jubilees (specifically Jubilees 10:4-5) can further
    illustrate the vast wicked influences of fallen angels through
    their demonic activities. These will find no mercy from the
    Almighty on the great day of judgment.

2. Baruch was actually the prophet Jeremiah's personal scribe
    in the days of the Jewish captivity (587 BC). The Book of
    Baruch (BOB) also was known, used, and read by the early
    church fathers.

3. There are New Testament Scriptures in which the writers borrow or even quote from the book of 2 Baruch. Luke 13:29 seems to quote 2 Baruch 4:37, John 3:13 seems to quote 2 Baruch 3:29, 1 Corinthians 10:20 seems to quote 2 Baruch 4:7, and 1 John 1:14 seems to quote 2 Baruch 3:37 or 38.

Although there are critics of these books, I am persuaded that there is no harm in using ancient writings that enhance and support already existing Scriptures from the King James canon. I find the descriptions of the throne of God and the second coming, especially, quite startling, and in some ways they open my imagination further to the glories of God.

APPENDIX B

The Amillennialist Position

Not all theorists believe in a literal new world order

Not everyone shares the belief in a physical new world order of Jesus Christ. Those who do not adhere to a literal thousand-year reign of Jesus upon the earth ruling from the temple are referred to as amillennialists. The prefix "a" in amillennialism means "no" or "not" –hence amillennial means *no millennium.* A belief in amillennialism holds that the thousand-year rule of Jesus Christ has already begun and is synonymous with the term *church age.* This view contends that Jesus will only appear at the final judgment (White Throne Judgment) and only then does He establish His reign on the new earth. This view also believes that Satan has already been bound and cast into the abyss and cannot deceive the nations.

I personally do not adhere to the amillennialists point of view because of the following four biblical indications:

1. It is clear that there are still evil influences that are tormenting the world and a satanic presence in world governments exists within most nations, if not all. Satan has not been thrown into the abyss thereby keeping him from deceiving the earth.

2. Like Charles Spurgeon, I feel that the Scriptures that describe the thousand-year millennial reign are too specific not be literal.

3. Jeremiah 23:5-8 says that during the millennial reign, the Messiah will execute justice and judgment on the earth. This has not happened symbolically or literally.

4. Isaiah, Ezekiel, and Amos clearly describe major earthly changes to the topography of Israel. This also has not taken place.

Amillennialism is historically based
upon anti-Semitic views

There is a disturbing influence of anti-Semitic sentiment found in the foundation of the amillennial doctrine. Theorists feel that a literal reign of Jesus from Jerusalem *is too Jewish*, with too much attention given to the house of Israel. Actually, amillennialism became widespread after the Council of Nicaea in 325 AD. The doctrine was drawn from this council and consequently spread into the Catholic church and soon-to-be Vatican, and even the Protestant movement. Both the Vatican (Catholicism) and Martin Luther (Protestantism) held serious anti-Semitic views. The establishment of a literal millennium, which places the Jews in a very strong reestablished Israel, became totally unacceptable to them. The literal thousand-year reign of Jesus Christ has a new world order that obviously uses Jews as leaders, regains tribal territory, ends the time of the Gentiles, and rebuilds the love and attention from God to the Jews.

As I mentioned in my book *"Meet the Beasts,"* The Vatican only officially recognized Israel as a nation in 2008. That is sixty some-odd years after Israel became a nation again in 1948. The Vatican established diplomatic relations with Israel only since 1993. The Vatican's position on Jerusalem is to make it an international territory, not a Jewish territory. The Vatican stated in 2010: "No promised land, no chosen people." So it is no wonder that the theory of amillennialism was propagated by the Catholic church and into Protestantism.

Early church fathers such as Justin Martyr and Eusebius both had doubts about the theology of John's book of Revelation, which propagates the renewed love for Israel and the Hebrews as the people of God. Further, many of the amillennial historians reject the writings of John in the book of Revelation because of the strong Jewish positioning during the millennial. The Jewish people hold that the second coming of the Messiah (which to them is the first

146

coming) will become the Jewish dream of regained Israel and Jerusalem becoming the capital of the world. The orthodox Hebrew is awaiting a Messiah who will destroy all of Israel's enemies and give them back their holy land.

Martin Luther was an anti-Semitic extremist thus spreading his hatred toward the Jews into Protestantism by way of ammillenialism. In his book *The Jews and Their Lies,* he gives his readers a written list of orders as to how to handle a Jew. He wrote this book in 1543, and wrote that all Jews should not be shown any mercy or kindness, no legal protection, and that we are all at fault for not slaying them. Here are a few extracts from his treatise of anti-Semitism:

> *"Firstly, to set fire to their synagogues or schools and to bury and cover them with dirt whatever will not burn... Second, I advise that their houses be razed and destroyed. Third, I advise that all their prayer books and Talmudic writings, in which such idolatry, lies, cursing and blasphemy are taught, be taken away from them. Fourth, I advise that their rabbis be forbidden to teach henceforth on pain of loss of life and limb. Fifth, I advise that safe-conduct be abolished on the highways completely for the Jews. Sixth, I advise that usury be prohibited to them, and that all their cash and treasure of silver and gold be taken from them and put aside for safekeeping."*

Martin Luther continues and advises that Jews should only be employed using their hands in hard labor careers. He calls them blind Jews, who are truly stupid fools. He writes that Jews are senseless people, and for all Christians to be on their guard against the Jews because they are from the den of thieves.

To conclude, it is no wonder that the doctrine of a physical one-thousand-year rule of Jesus Christ with a newly established Israel is too Jewish to be accepted by the leaders of the Vatican and the denominations that splintered off from Martin Luther's Protestantism.

About the Author

Pastor Frank Mazzapica was born in Boston, Massachusetts, and eventually moved to New York City during his high school years.

Simultaneously to serving more than nine years in the United States Air Force, Mazzapica began his ministry in January 1978. He accepted his first senior pastor position in 1983 at the age of twenty-six, and has since served the kingdom of God as a pastor, an evangelist, a marriage and family counselor, and an author of six books on an array of topics.

Mazzapica earned his master's degree in psychology and served in various public schools as a school counselor as well as an adjunct lecturer at Lamar University in Beaumont, Texas. He taught general psychology, adult development and aging, and child psychology.

Mazzapica is married to his wife, Leah, and has six children and four grandchildren. Presently he is the founder and senior pastor of New Covenant Church in Humble, Texas, a suburb of Houston.

Please feel welcome to contact the author at:

www.frankmazzapicaministries.com

www.newcc.org

Lightning Source UK Ltd.
Milton Keynes UK
UKOW06f0132010816
279599UK00001B/23/P